AWS

****

THE COMPLETE GUIDE FROM BEGINNERS TO ADVANCED FOR
AMAZON WEB SERVICES

ABOUT THIS EBOOK

Amazon Web Services (AWS) is an Amazon host Web platform that provides flexible, reliable, scalable, easy-to-use, and cost-effective solutions. This tutorial contains several important topics that illustrate how the AWS feature works and how it works to run a Web site in Amazon Web Services.

This Ultimate Guide eBook is meant for......

This tutorial is ready for beginners who want to learn how Amazon Web Services works to provide reliable, flexible, and cost-effective computer services to the cloud.

What You Must Have

To take advantage of this tutorial, you need to know how Amazon Web Services can help you extend your cloud computing service.

Table of Contents

INTRODUCTION

The almighty Amazon is not just a bookstore. They were one of the Pioneers of Internet marketing strategy to take big losses in their first year, using online affiliate sales to take advantage of a completely new marketing concept as the main engine of Selling their books on subtraction and other media products. Now they are in Black, one of the most successful online businesses and still changing the Internet around them as they hope the Internet is making sales and marketing changes. Best of all, they can help you earn money on small and large scales to support your business with their technical acuti or allow you to sell books to the affiliate commission from your own website.

While most people think of the books they think of Amazon site, their business model is no longer a day. They sold the books. In fact, most of their online toolkits have improved to support sales books: reviews, ratings, sales rankings, trusted product descriptions and photos, and preferred exclusive lists Traditional Tools such as customer service and delivery to purchase your ebooks online. They created the best website.

However, now you can find tens of thousands of other products, toys and baby products from traditional new book lines and initial options from used books to get the most impossible Repellent. Why are so many products? That's because Amazon doesn't sell them outright.

Amazon is actually becoming a clearing house for the major book sellers as well as other vendors. In 2001, after unsuccessful attempts to expand their line of books and other new media, they launched the Amazon market, the first used book to increase their new book lines. They have gradually expanded large arrays of their products today. Amazon Market is directly challenged in half site and EBay non-agricultural services; Customers are offered to buy as well as sold them that they want. And in its latest Amazon webshop additions, extending its service, you'll be able to run your own branded stores using their trusted ecommerce service.

If you are looking for access to Internet marketing, Amazon. may be the way to start becoming a partner. The Amazon partner is a customer-consumer affiliate. According to the Affiliate community (Amazon will say no), about 40% of Amazon's sales are driven by the affiliated sales.

Amazon. It is very easy to join a partner program at those with low fees. Fill out a short questionnaire on your site and they will send you instructions on how to get specific books and coded links to the product. (You can't send customers to the Amazon area.) Instead, promote specific books or items.) You are a commission that varies – the higher the price will be the higher the product rate, so you can make a healthy amount of Kindle, but do not spill the Peperback – and access the image and information about the item's sales. These feeds are not instant. You must store a minimum value and then pay on a quarterly basis.

If you are only on Internet marketing, running affiliate ads for Amazon products in your Web page are one of the best ways to get your feet wet. As a long-term business model, it's not very big, but Amazon increases the price of product and dollar sales time, and even after turning to big and good profits, the advertising value.

WHAT IS CLOUD COMPUTING?

Cloud computing is a term used to describe both the platform and the type of application. The cloud computer platform dynamically deploys, configures, configures and re-designs servers on demand. Cloud servers can be physical mechanisms or virtual machines. Additional clouds typically include other computer resources, such as storage area networks (SANS), network devices, firewalls.

Cloud computin also describes applications that have been expanded to make them available on the Internet. These cloud apps use large data centers and powerful servers that host Web applications and services. Anyone with a suitable internet connection and a standard browser can access the cloud application

A. Definition

Cloud is a set of virtualized computer resources. The cloud can:

• Hosting different work loads, including journaling-style archival jobs and interactive applications that the user encounters.

• Enable loads to deploy and scale fast with rapid construction of virtual machines or physical machines.

• Supports an unnecessary, self-repair, highly scalable programming model that allows loads to recover from very inevitable hardware/software failures

• Monitoring of the use of resources in real time so that appropriations can rebalanced

B. Cloud Computer against computer networks

Cloud environments Support Online computer by providing fast physical and virtual servers where Web applications can be accessed.

Cloud services should not be confused with a computer network [3]. A computer network involves splitting a large task into several smaller tasks running parallel to individual servers. Networks require multiple computers, usually thousands, and often use servers, desktops, and laptops. Clouds also support a network environment, such as three-dimensional WEB architecture that work in the standard or WEB 2.0 applications. The cloud is more than a collection of computer resources because the cloud provides a mechanism for managing these resources. Management includes securing, changing requests, rebooting, charging balancing, decompression, and control.

II. TYPES OF CLOUD SERVICE PROVIDERS

A. Software as a Service (SaaS) SaaS customers borrow a cloud service provider's infrastructure, such as Salesforce, to access items. Applications are typically offered to customers over the Internet and are fully managed by the cloud service provider. This means that managing these services, such as upgrade and repair, is the responsibility of the service provider. The great advantage of SaaS is that all clients use the same software version and a new SaaS feature, which all clients use the same version of the software, and new features can be easily integrated by the provider and are therefore available to all clients. Can easily be integrated by the retailer and is therefore available to all customers. The advantage of SaaS [4] is that all clients use the same version of the software, and new features can be easily integrated by the provider and are therefore available to all customers.

B. The platform-as-Service PaaS cloud provider provides an application platform as a service, such as Google's application Engine. This allows clients to deploy their own software using the tools and programming languages provided by the provider. Clients can control settings related to deployed applications and environments.

C. As with SaaS, the provider is responsible for managing the underlying infrastructure. Infrastructure as an IaaS service provides hardware resources, such as a processor, disk space, or network components, as a service. Typically, these resources are supplied by the cloud provider as a virtualization platform, and clients can access them over the Internet. Clients have full control over the virtualization platform and are not responsible for managing the underlying infrastructure.

D. Storage as a storage-as-a service (STaaS) is a business model in which large service providers lease space in a storage infrastructure based on a subscription. The economies of scale in the service infrastructure are much more costly to them than most individuals or companies can provide their own warehouse when considering the total cost of ownership. The storage-as-Service feature is typically used to troubleshoot offsite backup problems. Storage critics as a service point out that using Internet services for storage requires high network bandwidth.

E. Security as a service (SECaaS) is a business model in which large service providers integrate their security services into their corporate infrastructure on a subscription basis at a higher cost than most individuals or Companies can provide their own when considering the total cost of ownership. These security services typically include authentication, antivirus software, antimalware/spyware, intrusion detection, and security event management.

F. Data as a service Data-as-a-service (DaaS) is a cousin of software as a service. Like all family members of the "as-service" (aaS), the DaaS concept is such that the product (in this case the data) can be made available to users on demand, regardless of the geographic or organizational department of the provider and the consumer. In addition, the emergence of a service-oriented architecture (SOA) creates a real platform where data is immaterial. This development led to the recent emergence of a relatively new concept of DaaS. The Data provided as a service was initially used primarily for network devices, but is now increasingly used for business and is less common in organizations such as the United Nations.

G. Testing environment as a service: Testing environment as a service (TEaaS), sometimes referred to as "Custom test environment ", is a testing environment delivery model that has hosted software and centrally linked data (usually in the cloud service) and which Typically, users who use a high-end client can usually access a Web browser.

H. Background As A Service: Background as a service (BAAS), also called "Mobile backend as a service" (MBaaS), is a model for providing web and mobile application developers in a way to connect their applications to cloud storage in the background and also provide features such as manage Users, Push notifications and integration with social networking services. These services are provided using customized program kits (SDKs) and application programming interfaces (APIS). BaaS is a relatively recent development in cloud work, where most of the 2011 or later come from BaaS. The global BaaS market had an estimated value of $216 500 000 in 2012.

HOW CLOUD COMPUTING WORKS

Let's say you're an executive in a large company. A specific responsibility ensures that all employees have the right hardware and software for their work. Buying a computer for everyone is not enough - you also need to buy a software or software license to give your employees the necessary tools. Whenever there is a new rent, you should either purchase more software or verify that the current software license allows other users. It's so stressful to sleep with a pile of big money every night.

As soon as possible, there may be alternatives for executives like you. This application allows workers to sign in to web-based services that require all programs for their work. Remote computers owned by other companies operate everything from e-mail to Word processing to complex data analysis programs. This is called cloud computing and can change the entire computer industry.

There are significant work changes in cloud computing systems[5]. Local computers no longer have to do all the heavy work when running the application. The computer networks that make up the cloud handle this. Reduce hardware and software requirements on the user's side. The only thing you need to run a computing system in a cloud interface that can be as simple as a web browser is to manage the rest of your cloud-based network.

There is a good chance that you have already used some sort of cloud services. If you have an email account with a web-based email service like Hotmail, Yahoo! Mail or Gmail, you've had some experience with cloud services. Instead of using an e-mail client on your computer, you can remotely log on to your Web e-mail account. Your account is not software and storage on your computer – it's the service computer in the cloud.

Advantages of Cloud Computing

Cloud computing is quick, easy to meet and work with the potential to change the performance of your business by removing existing bottlenecks, enabling business operations to work with great resources, and enabling you to A lot of resources that can bring an IT infrastructure that has the potential to change performance. Access all the most up-to-date cloud technology.

Most modern companies know something about cloud computing these days, even if they're not yet involved in the business structure. They understand that this is a type of service that allows them to use apps and share Resources on the Internet. As services evolve and problems experience over time and are corrected over time, the cloud begins to attract the attention of home computer users as well as any other company.

The elimination of cloud hardware has made a huge impact on future internal bugs or solutions to deal with applications and other problems to get the space of the physical server and the software it needs to perform As a solution, it is positive for users. Let's continue to work with better services. Security is also the main point of sale for businesses, but now there are solutions to create your cloud's privacy level as effectively as security and standard reserved servers.

You can use a lot of the first software resources that take the necessary hardware and software to manage IT requirements, computer systems and networks for trading in any size. All basic aspects that may be less than the overall cost involved in executing a successful business - especially if a problem arises such as computer crashes, become a virus, or often consumes a lot of time and energy to experience a bad internet connection.

For cloud computing providers, this outsourcing is not accessible to high-tech and software prices, and is not specifically accessible to those without IT portfolios. There are many vendors to choose from, so make sure you find one that is known to be reliable – if you have a large customer base, you can show that a good provider will continue to be selected and selected. You are already very present looking around and asking questions - to find out how easy it is to use if they have good customer service, and you can provide your business needs.

The benefits of cloud computing are enormous for each company, and as you grow, whether it's a merger with another organization, expanding it to another city or another country, or a new advanced service that allows IT infrastructure to be used everywhere Produce the product line and whenever you need it. Consider IaaS, SaaS, Disaster or Backup Services to expand your business and get more financial benefits. This means that when you pay for the money you use, you can have the infrastructure you need for peak hours without paying in a short time.

Any company that still manually supports basic business data is wasting not only time and money, but not enough to become a disaster and existing applications must be unreliable. Cloud storage is about an hour, automatic online backup copy of important data, and, if necessary, allows it to be restored quickly.

Cloud hosting can relieve stress due to a computer backup failure, as if it continues to serve customers with minimal downtime if it causes the system to crack, using the latest technology to provide a 24-hour backup system Before secured important data through.

DISADVANTAGES OF CLOUD COMPUTING

Everyone has pros and cons. Ideally, cloud computing also includes a wide range of advantages, and has a number of shortcomings. Some of them are discussed below and will help you determine how much cloud computing will be your needs.

1. Privacy

Cloud computing makes all your personal data on servers. Not only emails, or social networking logs but everything is on a third-party server. The issue of privacy is the first to emerge. What is the third-party guarantee to users that their information is not guilty?

2. Security

Powerful servers like Hotmail, Yahoo and Picasa have enough security that protects not only their information but also their users. However, these cloud service vendors are relatively small and less vulnerable to external attacks. It puts a question mark on customer safety of malware such as viruses, worms, spyware and Trojan horses, as well as deliberate people to attack.

3. Surveillance

Do not perform various maintenance tasks such as checking the disk and unfragmenting the disk on your computer to keep it running efficiently? These tasks keep your computer healthy and give you a better user experience. Cloud Computing on the other hand, does not allow you to run any such check, you rely heavily on cloud service providers (CPS-Gold). In addition, the standard user has little knowledge of alternative methods used by SCPs such as those related to backup, recovery and recovery.

4. Transferable

Sometimes, the user runs cloud computing on a particular server, and finds that cloud service providers are not good enough, he or he lands in a crowded area. It is very difficult to switch to a different CSP. Next, all you can do is bring to the current bisbe defects.

5. Downtime

Think in a few seconds when one of the sites you want the most to visit shows a stopline. Unpredictable situation makes you panic and leaves no choice. Stopping a Cloud service provider is even more terrible because it prevents you from accessing your computer at all. No matter how confident the Web server is, it will not be completely safe from stop errors. Even some of the most famous and reliable sites have passed through the stops. For example, Amazon has seen a four-day long hiatus affecting millions of users as of February 21, 2011. On February 2, 2011, Gmail and Google+ had servers facing the same two-day problem that severely affected their users. Sony was also forced to close the PlayStation network for 25 days affecting 7,000,000 users on April 21, 2011 after an unauthorized interference account.

The above flaws should be considered before you make your decision throughout the transition in cloud computing. However, it should be noted that cloud computing is still evolving and will improve on time.

6 strategies for discovering Amazon web sites to expand your web business.

Amazon's official website became operational in 1995. In just two decades, the site has become the largest online reseller and retailer, with almost all types of products or services, including almost every category, as you might expect. It gives it a name, including products and services, but not limited to consumer electronics, retail articles, digital applications and content, custom labels and brands, cloud computing, content production, donations and charitable organizations.

Amazon began retailing books online. If you're thinking about starting your own startup, or if you want to take your existing business to the next level online, Amazon's success story will actually act as an ethical booster. It used to be a harmless start-up and now provides a platform for countless others. You can also join people who already use the Amazon platform to promote their online business, as well as others who have signed up for Amazon Club online membership.

Take stock of the following six strategies to best leverage the Amazon portal for business gains:-

1. Amazon: Promote your products or services - although Amazon is the largest online inventory of various products and services, it will be in good condition if you start with a single product or tying service, your 'Sell Amazon' program. After that, you can graduate to become a small seller with more than 10 items. In addition to monthly fixed fees, you pay a fixed percentage or amount for each sale. In return, you'll get the benefits of using management, creative, and technical tools to explain your revenue.

2. Use the Amazon platform as your advertising platform: - You can use the website to list your product pictures with clear product details and 'How... Instructions. This promotional model is much cheaper than using a program

that sells on Amazon, with a pay-per-click (PPC) basis. With adware, as much detail as possible is required for your product or service.

At least you don't have to continue uploading price lists, inventory lists, and other details.

3. You can turn your online store into a big store: - Amazon gives you the opportunity to open an 'online store' if you are a green corner and therefore have no experience in online marketing. This is your own virtual store.

4. Use Amazon's Compliance Policy: - The best way to promote and sell through Amazon is to take full responsibility for safely delivering products to customers, handling returns, and providing customer support.

5. Take advantage of Amazon data storage and cloud computing services: - In addition to using the Amazon portal as an advertising and sales platform, you can also take advantage of web installations to store your files or valuable business data.

6. Use Amazon Purchase: - No matter what online platform you use to promote your product or service, you can always benefit from Amazon's purchase as an alternative to the customer' payment.

GETTING STARTED WITH AMAZON WEB SERVICE

Public Versus Private Clouds Computing

1. Amazon, if your first cloud computer provider, provides the public Computer – Anyone can use it.

2. Most organizations, reflect on this new Amazon new website, asked why they can't create and deliver a service like AWS to users, hosted by their respective documents. This premise has become known as the personal computer.

3. As the system continues, several hosting stewards consider that their clients can give a segregated part of their data plan and let customers build out there. This principle can also involve individual computer because it is dedicated to a user. Conversely, because the information that comes from one-on-one contact group is the personal thing?

4. Lastly, when a bulb is coming out that the group cannot choose between public or private, the hybrid language created to refer to the company using both private and public environments.

If you continue your journey in the cloud, you'll probably experience hopeless discussion about which of these particular cloud environments is the better option. My own position is that generic cloud computing will surely become an important part of the organization's environment, no matter where you stand on the private/public/Hybrid issue. Besides, Amazon will almost certainly be the biggest provider of generic cloud computing, so it makes sense to plan a future that includes AWS. (Reading this book is part of this planning effort, so you get a golden star for being well on your way!)

Understanding Amazon Philosophy of Business

Amazon Web Services was formally revealed to the world by 13 March 2006. On that day, AWS offered a simple storage service, its first service. (As it could be imagined that simple storage services were shortly shortened to S3.)

The idea behind S3 is simple: it can be network, a setting, anyone can put an object-basically, any bundle

Byte S3. These bytes can include digital photos or backup files or package, video or audio recording or spreadsheet file or well, you get the idea.

S3 is relatively limited at the beginning. Although the subject may, can not understand, from anywhere to write or read, they only have region: United States. Additionally, the object cannot be larger than 5Gigabyte-Small in any way, but surely much less files, those who may want to store in S3. The operation can be used for objects as well quite limited: You can write, read, delete them, and that's it.

Measuring The AWS Setting

Amazon is a pioneer in cloud work and lives under a stone that we've never heard of a cloud, so being a pioneer in this industry is a big deal. The question is if AWS is a big dog on the market and that's the hottest computer job, how big is the one from the way we talked about it? This is an interesting question, because Amazon has revealed little of the scope of trade. Instead of splitting the revenue from AWS, you will want to group it into other financial report categories. However, we have some clue to its size based on information from the company itself and information from industry experts. Amazon itself provides a proxy for the growth of AWS services. Often the number of objects stored in the S3 service is reported. Figure 1-1 shows how the number of objects stored in the S3 system skyrocked from 2 900 000 000 at the end of 2006 to over 2 000 000 000 000 to the end of the second quarter of 2012 and grows at a huge pace. Given this pace of growth, it is clear that trade is doing well. There are additional estimates of the size of the AWS service. A very clever consultant named Huan Liu researched the AWS IP address and estimated the total number of server racks that AWS maintains based on estimates of the number of servers in the switchboard. Table 1-1 displays

Table 1-1   **Total AWS Servers**

numbers by region.

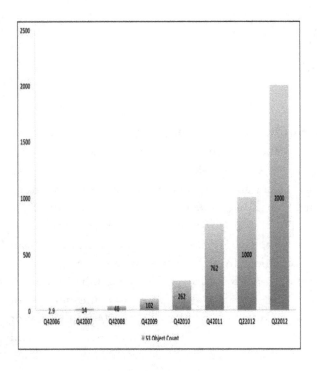

AWS Region	Number of Server Racks	Number of Servers
US East	5,030	321,920
US West (Oregon)	41	2,624
US West (California)	630	40,320
EU West (Ireland)	814	52,096
AP Northeast (Japan)	314	20,096
AP Southeast (Singapore)	246	15,744
SA East (Brazil)	25	1,600
Total	**7,100**	**454,400**

AMAZON WEB SERVICE-PLATFORM

Services that provide additional application functionality: For a secondary test, the simple Thor service of Amazon (SQS) provides functionality that enables acetone communication between your application and its users, or perhaps another application. . I call it an extended bathroom.

The main but generally COM-Plex are the traditional software offering the trade weed for additional applications: an example of the intelligence application launched the latest red Shift business. Many of the vendors have built this place, and their applications have two common characteristics: they cost a lot, and they are difficult to use. The transition is designed to simplify the construction and activation of a business intelligence application and make it a lot less expensive to implement.

AWS Management tools: Useful for managing API-specific AWS services and AWS management Console (for example, for ECS events), but they did not provide much help for managing AWS resources that could cause an application. How do I set up and manage a group of resources in an application? Amazon offers three separate tools: elasticity, Phenesti, Cloud, and OpsWorks. You need to understand the differences between them so that you can choose the right person.

AWS platform services offer the same benefits (and generate the same probes of the Leams) as the basic services. Although given to them useful, easy to use functionality at a reasonable price, they have the potential to lock up--it's almost impossible to invest a number of resources in a solution. In fact, the potential for the lockdown is high for a platform of cheese-visas, as they are closely related to ecological environments than debated in Chapter 8. So, the benefits you receive by accepting these services, you must carefully assess whether there are any concerns that you might have about the conclusion.

Search by Cloud Search

Search is one of the most useful features online, and huge companies are built to look for. (Have you ever heard of Google?) However, not all searches need to cover the entire internet, and all searches should not be public. For example, you can set the contents of a company Web site to be searchable or restrict who can view search results.

For many companies that want to use search on websites or other content repositories, the challenge is that the quality of common search tools related to content management systems is boring, terrible. For companies that want to create content containers, the situation is worse if they have a large collection of documents that have been deleted in the file system instead of the actual content management System (searchable). The search mechanism cannot use these ENVI-ronments data (regardless of how faulty).

In general, the options were not attractive if you wanted to use advanced search features, which were usually included in the content management system, or that were included in the chaotic content store.

You can purchase expensive patented search software and use it to configure content search features. This option requires large financial and sial expenditure and is relevant only for high value content.

Download and use the open source search software, which is both Capa-BLE cheaper. This option is not great, but the search function makes searching for economically viable content that is more useful.

The Downside Is Still

Locate the hardware that is used to install the search software. You may need to purchase devices that support the search software.

Install and configure the search software for the purchased hardware. You should have more information about the search software. Most people have little expertise in this view, but it is inevitable if you want to enable content search.

Manage your hardware and software and make sure your search software is still running. As the content repository grows to a point where the index grows according to its originally purchased hardware, it returns to the same (unattractive!) to purchase the hardware and configuration software routines that you started.

Of course, the situation is not satisfactory, and it matures confusion. Amazon launched CloudSearch at the beginning of 2012. Cloud Search

Amazon is based on the technology it uses on its own website, which should represent its functionality and scalability.

CloudSearch is based on the A9, a search company that Amazon inckubate years ago, and realized that search and search capabilities are important to your business. A9 is used to search Amazon and its affiliates. Initially, A9 focused on text search and related results, but the A9 technical team relied on the user's interaction with the branch image and social search, a class that adds con text to regular text searches.

CloudSearch can search for structured content, such as Word Pro-cessing files and structured content, commonly referred to as structured Web page or forum publication collections, such as free text or text.

CloudSearch function is relatively simple, but it is somewhat tricky to understand. The content you want to search must be indexed (content data is evaluated so that individual words can be used). For example, if you want to search for a large number of DOCU-ments Zoo, you need to crawl the word elephant so that the search software can recover all documents containing the word elephant.

You can download the data you want to search in the domain where the name of the given domain is the name of the searchable document database. For data download, cloud search uses forces for self-defense (short for formatting search data). Although you can create SDF on the fly for certain types of data, such as PDF and Word files, for others you need to create SDF documents on their own in order to upload your data. SDF documents can be formatted either in XML or JSON-two common criteria to describe datasets. The SDF record is nothing more than a coordinated set of elements with a fundamental value describing the data that you want to be able to search for.

After downloading SDF documents, the cloud search analyzes them and creates indexes for all the items you specified that you want to be able to search for them. For example, if you create a set of SDF documents that identify all players in a particular year's sports, you can search the position you played or the number of games played during the year. The cloud search creates indexes in all the fields that you have selected as a search. You can then perform searches against your domain in the fields that you identified as a search.

You should also create an access policy that is similar to EC2 SECU groups. You can define the IP addresses that you want to allow access to cloud search, both for access to search and for administrative access to the domain. (Usually, allow all IP addresses to search through cloud search, because the most common situation is to allow Web site visitors to search for information on the site, but you can restrict access to searches for your company's employees or multiple Partners.)

Although you can perform searches from a control block managed by the operating system, the most common search is performed by if you are adding a search to a website, you can use the API method to conduct searches in your cloud search.

Tools for the searched search

Cloud Search maintains a high level of performance by supporting all indexes that you have created within EC2 instances. Now, the obvious question is exactly how many cases will you EC2 the search box to? However, this number is not controlled; Cloud Search supports the dimensions of the three copies: small, large and very large. If necessary, the cloud search divides the domain indexes into multiple instances to keep them in memory and to support fast searching.

Scope Of The Cloud Search

The searched domain regional search that affects where you post the domain lookup. If the Web site that you enabled using cloud Search is in a specific area, there will be no charge for network traffic if the domain search is located in the same area. Of course, since the cloud Search can be accessed via the OS API, searches can be performed from anywhere on the internet, as well as in other axis regions.

Cost Of Searching

The price per hour is as follows:

Little search: $. 10 per hour

Great demand: $. 39 per hour

Great additional search: $. 55 per hour

Controlling Video Conversion With an Elastic Transcoder

Elastic Transcoder, a relatively new service (launched in 2013), is conceptually quite simple: converts video files from one format to another.

Video transcoding is a widely applied computing task. You must have lived under a rock so you wouldn't notice the video was everywhere. Although people have been using special video recorders for more than 40 years, the growth of smartphones (initiated since the launch of the iPhone in 2007) is an overcharged video trend. Activated by iPhone and, more recently, the iPad, smartphones with video devices and tablets are flooded in the market. Amazon even provides a family of tablets branded light fire. Each of them is now a video recorder.

It also underlined the ease of sharing videos through video hosting services. By the time this book was written, 72 hours of video were uploaded to YouTube every minute of the day. Although it may seem now and then all 72 of these hours are with cats in fun or heart videos, the truth is that the video is now a communication medium used by all kinds of provide for all kinds of purposes – entertainment, education, Documentation, evidence and a thousand water-purifying RS.

For many video creators, this video explosion is a nuisance of wealth-so many output devices are available, each of which has its own preferred format, which make all the necessary versions of the video to support the preferences of The customer is a challenge. Thus, transcoding – converting one video format to another – is now a critical opportunity to capture video sites. Being able to take a video source and prepare all the versions needed for widely used displays devices is now critical for organizations that want to capitalize on the power of visual communication.

It's been part of a transcoding mix for a long time. In fact, when Netflix first launched its video streaming service, it went as part of its video-transcoding strategy. It combines with video transcoding is a natural fit: S3 is a great choice for storing original and transcoding versions of video, and EC2 can naturally host the transformation process. There are no statistics available to show what percentage of SIA's total load is represented by video transcoding, but probably a significant part.

The load associated with transcoding may be unstable – in fact, depends on the organization and type of videos it creates, transcoding of loads can vary as much as 1 000 percent over a period of time. If your organization uses the LAWS to transcoding goals, the service may be fecal in terms of ease of access, but such very variable workloads impose significant management challenges. Translation? Most likely you will need to grow and shrink your EC2 processing pool quite a bit to meet the requirements for transcoding.

Given these facts, the launch of the elastic Transcoder is pre-conclu: It helps organizations to perform useful video transcoding in YUANJIA, but removes overhead management costs.

Elastic Transcoder, which is designed to simplify common transcoding tasks, allows you to specify videos that need to be transcoding and automatically pulls individual videos from S3 storage, performs a transcoding operation, and Then insert a version of the S3 storage location.

Using elastic Transcoder, you can specify the features of the output format you want for your videos, although it also provides a number of preconfigured popular output formats for the iPhone, iPad, and, of course, Kindle Fire.

You can manage the elastic Transcoder from the management console are, but also offers a relaxed interface so that applications can call the service yourself. The relaxed interface is likely to represent most of the use of services because many online video applications will switch to elastic Transcoder, given the ease of use. Amazon provides language SDK (software development kits) in a number of languages, such as Python and PHP, to reduce the burden for developers; Instead of having to call directly to the

Each transcode work presented on the elastic Transcoder is presented as a JSON object containing the name of the bucket that holds the file to be transcoding, a set of configurations that you want to apply to the file (the output formats you want, Example), and the location when the transcoding video is placed.

Elastic Transcoder Works Very Easily.

Identify the video that you want to convert.

Create an elastic translator conveyor or use an existing conveyor. In this context, the pipeline is the service endpoint to which the job is sent. Because your AWS account can have several different conveyors, you can allocate and prioritize transcoding tasks as needed.

There is, however, only one pipeline. This step allows for elastic transcoder access to resources (e.g. video files on the S3 bucket) to run transcoding services.

If the elastic transcoder does not have the corresponding rights, you will not be able to access the resource and perform transcoding. (Optional) Create a preset that contains the settings you want to apply to the elastic translator during the transcoding process.

If you are using an existing conveyor, you can use an existing preset or create a new one.

Amazon offers presets that support common transcoding operations, such as formats for the iPhone, which can be used instead of creating their own presets.

You can create a job that represents a specific video transcoding operation. The work is presented in JSON notation. When the service was first started, each output format demanded a different job. Currently, work can request multiple outputs, reducing the cost of network transfer slightly.

(Optional) You use the AWS Instant Messaging Service (SNS) to configure the elastic transcoder to provide status updates when the job runs.

When the transcoding job is complete, do something by using the output video recorded in the S3. You can load video objects configured in the S3 Bucket or allow access to the video objects in the bucket (you can also use the appropriate access control on the list [ACL] setting to give access). You can also configure the S3 Bucket to act as the CloudFront origin of the bucket and the cache video of the AWS CloudFront endpoint.

An elastic transporter must be used. Amazon processes the service Management queues (pipelines), the service instance where the service is running, and the service to send the work. You are only responsible for managing the original video files, communicates with the elastic transcoder, and manipulating the output of video files. In other words, elastic transcoders can benefit from the process of transcoding video without having to manage the details. The elastic transcodr scope of the elastic transcoder is regionally scoped: Individual pipelines are available in one area, but the service has a RESTful interface and is linked to accounts in other regions. You can use the S3 bucket. During this book, the elastic Transcoder is not available in all AWS areas, but Amazon is soon you can expect that transcoder is available.

Elastic transcoderi Cost Elastic Transcoder offers a very simple cost Model: AWS pays a fixed price per minute transencoded video. For standard definition (SD) videos, the cost is about $. 015 per minute. The cost of high-definition (HD) video is about $30 per minute.

The cost is slightly higher in some areas, but the SD transcoding (at that time in writing) does not cost more than $. 018 per minute, and the price of HD transcoding does not exceed $. 036 per minute. Amazon offers free use of the elastic translator. Every month, the first 20 minutes of SD transcoding, or the first 10 minutes of HD transcoding, are Pro-vivid free.

Simple Queue Service

It's time for my favorite AWS service: a simple queue service. (This is the geeky choice, I know – but what can I say?) A queue is an incredible system that is very useful in applications that designer-Unfordot because you have set the risks, applications that cannot be repaired if they are Nate to the services integrated.

So, if you don't doubt your excitement about the queue, what's it all about? The attitude is that death is easy to understand: it is a conversation element in the two processing resources that will allow them to perform tasks that do not need to process synchronously. This narrative may be quite difficult, but the reality is that you use queues in real life all the time.

Tell me you need your shirt. You can go to the clean service, hold onto your shirt, wait until the service moves and keep going, and take them home. This is one way to do this, but I think you agree that the size of your time is wasting so much. You can refer to these operating systems as synchronous: You are calling the pure service, and you will expect it to be complete.

Another way to purge your shirt-and the ability to make this service a universively worldwide – that is to take your shirt in underwear, drop it down, and get a ticket for the time you undo them , go to other projects (which may include dropping your shoes in a shoe repair area to get new heels), and then back up to the date of the ready-to-be-willing to pick up your shirt well , healthy, and clean.

This second character is asynchronous. You don't have to be forced to wait for your ready-to-be shirt – just put it in your laundry service in the queue and get a ticket that will be used in order to check your job. You came back for a time, and your work was promised clean, as you went out and made the second (reliable) miracle work.

The queue is the best tool for work done in a service without requiring a call to wait for the results. Elastic transcoder, AWS service I booked first in part "Video Manager conversions with Elastic transcoder, " It's a good example. Many applications can be used with video transcoding not to wait for transcoding projects to complete. Imagine a home web site where you can upload video and then

Allows guests for simple formats such as iPhone, iPad, Kindle Fire or Web Access. If you're using a website, you don't want to be forced to wait until the video is transcoded, right? Especially because the other figures were shown to other people, there was no point for people to wait for the transcoding act of Plete. The video can be supplied and placed in a queue that is not reencoded, and leaves the designer to do something else (for example, monitoring the rest of the web).

Many, many of the components of the processing correspond to the implementation of the asynchronous Pattern; As I describe my attitude of love to confess, there is no doubt to use it sometimes and not being exploited by the use of designers who are so bad.

Simple Service Queue

SQS You can create an access queue for AWS and then set the load data in that queue. However, you can also specify the queue-based access to access only the wider range from your account. The ability to allow a wider number to be used as a queue is useful if you want to allow outside the status of a non-restricted group (tell your company's partners) or the members of the service to be able When they get – in particular, the performance of your application requires the designer to wait until the task is complete.

In fact, Amazon has provided the SQS as strong as its uptime, which leaves some of the most natural systems, which may affect the production of the SQS. You have to know that your work with SQS to make sure you don't take amazing service habits.

SQS allows multiple information senders and retrieve to share queue, which is a strange way to show that a queue allows multiple processes to put messages in queue and delete them. For example, you can manipulate multiple AWS instances that are designed to retrieve video uploads from elastic transcoders so that large jobs in the queue do not delay encoding requests.

One way Amazon can make SQS robust is that it implements redundant queues in the background; If a queue fails, the second mirrored queue may run concurrently until the failed queue is restarted. This policy ensures that all resource failures cannot make SQS unavailable.

However, because messages can be transmitted across redundant resources, they cannot be delivered in the order that is placed in the queue. Unlike some other queue products, SQS does not guarantee the first-in-first-out delivery (FIFO). If the submitter splits the job into multiple messages, the recipient cannot ensure that they are retrieved in the correct order.

Even for many queue-based applications, there is no guarantee that delivery commands will not be a problem, those requiring a requested message sequence must create a superqueue coordination mechanism; But for these applications, you need to create a superqueue coordination mechanism. The serial number that is part of the queue message is correct. A message submitter that places multiple messages belonging to a single population job can place a serial number in the first message, a total Mes-sage number 3, and a message that instructs the reader that his MA message gets three completed commits. The receiving application will read the total message number in the first message, stating that it requires three messages to get full commit and continue reading until messages 2 and 3 are retrieved. Despite the lack of FIFO mechanism. Amazon guarantees that each message will be delivered at least once. Before retrieving the message, which remains in the queue, waiting for the read.

If no browser requests a message, the ability to keep the message before reading the message may cause problems. If this happens frequently, the queue can be backed up by unread messages, and there will be enough unread messages, and even AWS will be overloaded. Therefore, SQS has a message timeout period that defines the length of time to keep messages in the queue. The default retention period is set to four days, which can be adjusted to meet the requirements of the program.

SQS How

The SQS is rezionaly in it. Each queue relates to a particular area. When you create queue SQS, you describe the AWS area of the queue. However, because SQS is a service given to AWS, you do not need to place it in a separate area. In fact, Amazon is the SQS of every queue of a dangerous place to get a robustness and prevent our success in the event that goes into an area where the number is available.

SQS the price

SQS the lack of money 50 SQS of applications, including application, is a type SQS API. This means that the dispatch, the queue and the setting of such qualities also require additional responsibilities. Of course, accepting is a retrieval prevalence of SQS API, so they are the source of a real price. For 10 posts (if they are less than a 64KB message), it can adebayo be considered an entry.

SQS also low to use; For 1 million SQS, you have a request for each month.

Keep in mind that we also pay the traffic sent from AWS, starting with the $. 12 every time Gigabyte and dropped as a better road, they were shipped. The first Gigabyte of traffic is within a month of a year

Using SQS

I hope the way you SQS and an overview of Piken service you are interested in using it. Queues are essential and SQS is a good, healthy and healthy one.

The worst challenge for most people in using queues is to consider how to practice the application. Instead of the growth serial in practice, where a work should be performed in the previous activity, consider how two works need to be done so they can communicate and warn them if they work.

By using queue to avoid all the waiting, you give a better experience-which is important. I urge you to use live by SQS to see how you can partition how to get the Indepen-Dent systems that use queues to send responsibility and to work. Once you've used queues, you'll find opportunities to use them and see many of the decisions you make.

Simple and straightforward work

According to the word a simple entry (ETC) what does it mean by acting on something that is in a way to a person or program the one computer just an interesting thing.

The simplicity of this definition, however, is the power of the judge. Consider the types of administrators who are responsible for the AWS application. It is clear that if something is not used properly, they should recognize them immediately.

One way to make the administrator who knows the challenge is to be logged in to AWS at all times, to justify the status of the second coming (not effective or fun).

Another way is to use a visitation: After a person describes at least one situation that someone should know (and presumably replies to), create here to answer the situation (and). Since each of these situations reads one of the errors that will occur in the context, one or more of the challenges is to send an example of someone or more to evaluate the problem and decide whether to act.

By Preview

I hope the foregoing is clear that it is essential. On the other hand, they do bongokely activities, and if a lot is sent, they can manage many jobs. Is The voice as a perfect opportunity for the AWS, the truth? You are right.

The work is AWS as a service mission that you create in your account. After you have created service, you are ready to begin the prophetic section.

SNS View

I hope the above clarifies that notifications are extremely useful. On the other hand, they have a decent amount of work to be created, and if you're sending a large volume of notifications, it might be a lot of work to manage. Sounds like a perfect opportunity for her, right? You're right.

SNS works as a service created in your account. After the service is created, you are ready to start distributing notifications.

You can – and probably will – have multiple notification streams in the notification service. You can have one stream for events and messages from your application to the system administrator, which notifies you of possible problems with your application. You can have an additional stream of notifications to send messages to users of your application. Almost certainly you will not want to mix messages for these two very different listeners who can read the notification messages intended for the other.

This list describes your choices for who gets topic information:

Individuals: You may identify based on certain personal policies in your account that are allowed to send or receive notifications. SNS is the identity and control of inte-bergrated and AWS access (i) managing personal SNS identity.

Account: You can identify the AWS account which can act as general regarding a particular topic. AWS account identifiers are used to show accounts that can do as Major for topics SNS.

Public: You can allow anyone to act as large for your SNS topic. It can be a bad idea for people who can send information, but it can be a good purpose to allow anyone who likes in a topic provided to receive information. Although my example SNS now focuses on technical staff who may need to receive notifications (such as system administrators), you can like a large audience of people who aren't part of your account telling about that event . A clear example is to send an email to all customers who tell you about your company offering — you will only keep the information at once, and then everyone will sign up to receive information.

Simple Flow Service

The simple Work Flow service (SWF) addresses a common challenge for large, distributed applications: How to coordinate all work between the application's COM-pandals, and specifically the success of the work carried out by a component to another Completion of the equipment's work. SWF will provide a service business for Amazon Imple for its own, internal operations. SWF is a powerful service, but I'll tell you that the initial letter of the shorthand (s simple) is not accurate. Unlike most AWS services, SWF is not easy to understand or use. On the other hand, the issues that are designed to address Swaf are badly complicated and undoubtedly require a sophisticated tool to master them.

Managing a complex workload is a traditional way to make a man do it. A person is doing a job, waiting for it to be complete, starting a second career, waiting for it to be done. The process has a couple of very basic issues: it's slow, it's boredom. It doesn't even scale well.

Another method used in the past is to write a custom work flow via scripting or code. That approach certainly does address the challenges of the pre-American system, but it has its own challenges. It supports the flow of work that is designed, but you have another kind of work flow, well, you are out of luck. Or you're trying to make your custom task flow public and pretty quickly work full time trying to maintain your simple work-flow product rather than make any... You know, work.

SWF Overview

SWF is a common flow organizer, commonly called a working machine. To use it, you create these two elements:

Tester: Defines the tasks to integrate with your flow

Tasks: Perform the work coordinates of the teacher

Although the SWF needs to be run on AWS (which is an AWS service, OK?), these tasks are not defined only for running within the ECS. They run wherever they can. In fact, they don't even run — a task can be a human-power thing. For example, if you enable a print job, a task can review the evidence for the user, which is a face-to-face task. After receiving positive feedback from the user, the printer employee can open a Web page, click the Approved button for the Review Certificate task, and continue with the rest of the workbook automatically. The working flow does not have to be a series of tasks; It can handle real tasks with parallel running. The flow may include a work relative level, in which a particular task cannot start until the previous tasks have completed successfully.

MANAGING AWS SERVICES

The chapter title I chose should be caused by obvious problems: given that you can use AWS property. Why do the AWS management console (detailed in Chapter 3) detailed in the opening chapter of this guide and the first chapter of this guide require additional administrative services?

This is a trick question in response to aws' property collections that are required to manage. In the past, you had to create or run apps, but you had to perform tasks that were not directly related to app functionality, such as installing and sorting software components and connecting them to other soft components. After the relationship was raised and it worked, you browsed his components, kept them on the run, reacted when the resource failed and brought them back. It was like every time you got into the store, you need to build a new car and clean the road. Just get a piece of milk!

An innovative aspect of AWS is that Post installs and manages components when it comes to using them. The good idea for AMAZON was to turn off automatic scans for the infrastructure so that we could focus on the features.

Why do you need sophisticated AWS management? Well, because the management effort has now changed the level. Manage the software components and make sure they work well.

Together, now you need to manage your products and make sure they play well together. The rest of this chapter provides some strategies for achieving this.

MANAGING AWS APPS

In some cases, ec2 assumes that you have written an application that you want to use SQS to talk about your order, insert an S3 entry, and download it. Well,

Amazon facilitates the creation of these resources, it is relatively simple to merge S3 buckets for use with EC2 order. But it is a big but lonely example. What happens when I cancel and restart a case? Well, I need you to order and reconnect to the S3 bin. What should I do if my app is very successful? Then you need to connect more cases, and these cases will restart... Well, you got the picture. He looks a lot like Mickey Mouse as a disciple of the wizard in "Disney movie Fantasia." or Classic references like Siszphus, rolling rocks endlessly from the top of the hill and rolling the plains. In other words, it's a bunch of repetitive tasks. They make mistakes, meaning you'll probably break their variables while trying to do what you need to do.

Doing infinite things can lead to new problems. If you can find something that controls the AWS side, you can make sure that your application has the right code, that other services can automatically fool each other and see if everyone should meet. Application?

The good news is something. In fact, Amazon offers three AWS Mananerian services designed to remove specific segments of users and better manage AWS' apps.

This section covers all three of these services, so you can understand the nature of these services and know when to use them. However, before you learn more about indieball services, you want to learn more about other AWS services: cloud and auto-sizing.

"AWS" Display Cloud

The cloud is an AWS component that monitors AWS resources. (Hot Advisor: Can also be used to monitor AWS apps.) Reporting. Get the injection? -- Provide information to users in the form of data and alerts above AWS resources. You can analyze or manipulate data, such as numer-IC exits, or directly access data, such as more intermediate types of data or data, such as graphics.

What kind of surveillance did I mean? A good example is the load of EC2 instances. You can let CloudWatch know about the processor load for EC2 instances. If the processor load percentage is higher than a certain level, or even triggers a programming action, such as autoscale events, the metric can be configured to generate e-mail alerts. (In the next section of this chapter, autoscale will be descaled.)

That's good, isn't it? Need more indicator examples? The following is a list of some other AWS features that cloud monitoring can monitor. CloudWatch tracks metrics over time, noting that many predefined metrics capture data every 5 minutes, but you can choose another interval as needed. All of these metrics are free, except for the first one;

Anyway, here's the list:

EC2 Instances: 10 metrics preselected every 5 minutes

Amazon EBS volume: 8 pre-selected metrics every 5 minutes

Elastic load Bale: 10 pre-selection indicators, 1 minute interval

Amazon RDS DB Instances: 13 pre-selected metrics every 1 minute

Amazon SQS Queue: 8 Pre-Select metrics every 5 minutes

Amazon SNS topics: Four metrics preselected every 5 minutes

Amazon ElastiCache nodes: 29 pre-selected metrics at 1-minute intervals

Amazon DynamoDB Table: Seven indicators preselected every 5 minutes You can also configure custom metrics to be monitored by CloudWatch.

In this relatively simple process, using the metrics to monitor to make a PUT API call, CloudWatch starts monitoring it for you. CloudWatch stores your data for two weeks, allowing you to track metrics over an extended period of time.

Of course, if you want to extend your duration for tracking purposes, you can use the API to extract data from CloudWatch and store it in another location. CloudWatch is enabled when you create an account. After that, simply select the metric you want to crawl on, and then use the build metric as needed.

For example, you can:

Extract metric data from the cloud monitoring API

Extract metric data from the Cloud Monitoring SDK

View metric data in the management console

Notify someone of metrics (or manage something like that in a process or log) Set an alert and then cause something to happen (for example, terminating a non-postback instance and launching another instance)

The auto climbing AWS phenomenon

The automatic scale of the AWS function is designed to solve a large problem: as having the correct number of instances EC2 can withstand the load on the application at some point.

In fact, you have several options to make sure you have the necessary number of opportunities to run at any time:

Wait for complaints to users. Issues to do often come from sufficient resources, and the ungifted users in Iaplay-cation can be a great way to identify an issue. Of course, when you run the risk of users after you refuse to contact your application that can be a bit see tragic if your company relies on iaplay-cation to generate profits.

Keep administrators of the hyperwatching system on Payroll. This person can continue to monitor the application of acceptable results. This costly strategy, in addition to the natural tendency of human behaviour to lose infrequently, although the cost circumstances are high, will almost be solved by this problem.

248 part III: Using AWS

Monitoring tracking to notify you about the operations issues. You can install your monitoring system, or the DNS lever old service, as described. Although this procedure solves the mistakes of the consumer complaint and all the solution administrators for the boring system, it still leaves you at the position (after I'm aware of the problem), having to execute a lot of the Manual work to react at all times, when the application isn't working properly. Better, yes, but not best.

A better solution is that the program will monitor itself and when further EC2 cases are required, automatically launch additional opportunities and connect them to the pool of calculation immediately, all without human Intervention.

Guess what? This solution ay-AWS automatic scaling. In short, automatic scaling allows you to determine how your app responds to changing the conditional load. The idea is that, beginning (or stopping) the cases at the right time, you can ensure that only the correct number of instances is the execution to support the application load.

The automatic scale works by adding an instance or reducing a group of running instances through the factors that you specify. Auto scaling takes care of activities related to cessation or executing an instance

This will automatically create the right instance settings and add it to the pool.

For a simple concept of automatic scalability, it is highly complex. Luckily, Amazon cares for most to efficiently manage its own configuration of automatically scaling in a simple way.

AWS uses the following elements to implement auto-sizing:

Start configuration: The settings Here are what you need to run the opportunity correctly. Think of it as a definition that applies to "Blank " to convert it to an instance that is valid in your app. The factors you want to set as startup settings have the AMI ID; Important Security pair (s); Security groups; and EBS volume (s) to be added to the specimen.

Scaling Group: This definition applies to a set of instances that have been initiated with a specific startup configuration. The Auto zoom group defines items, such as minimum and maximum instances, where a program must have. Therefore, you always want to have two operational opportunities to ensure accessibility, but you don't want to have more than five to avoid leftover costs.

Plan scaling: the Sizing determination for what are generally sizing groups respond to assign workloads. The goal should be dynamic (DVR to the list such as crowded and load response group) or for more predictable, it is best if you need to group people hours before a expected event (such as mission sizing to make sure evidence is designed to provide a renewal time every day D, when finances all week if analyzed for vine-pany).

After the best protection currently does not work, let it begin sizing uses in some areas and deploy the cross between them. This ensures that even offline the entire area, you can visit.

Here is a question for sure: If there are more instances can run within the, how will you format them? The table of contents or slack sizing will associ-ated with a flexible load balancer, which can be spread in any time of the group. As a person attack and begin to receive a sizing, the vehicle sizing to help manage the information in the application configuration with immediately available load-balance (or write).

AWS Operating Services

AWS Operations is Amazon's latest addition to its library management tools and was released in March 2013. While you can reasonably ask why AWS needs another management tool that comes with AWS, I can think of three reasons: AWS customers want better support for the entire lifecycle of your application.

They want this to be particularly useful for incremental development and a faster transition to production, which is now a typical application. Other AWS management tools, represented by elastic Beanstalk and the cloud, tend to assume that the application code to be deployed is static and complete. A new process and tool IT file was developed to reduce the need for application deployment.

The practice is DevOps, a word or mash-up of connections (combinations), and if you prefer, it is recommended that you integrate development and operations to simplify the entire lifecycle of your application and reduce the time required to convert applications. Some open source products have become an important part of the DevOps movement, and one of the chefs is part of OpsWorks.

While many technical employees are very satisfied with the work of text and API-based tools, many will find it easier to use visualization tools to implement complex tasks. Let's face it - JSON (especially COM-plexJSON files, such as the files required for cloud formation) is challenging, at least. To meet these requirements, Amazon will release OpsWorks, a one-man age tool designed to support complex multi-tier applications during their deployment lifecycle (check), integrated with the chef (check!)) and provides an interface to manage vision (check and finish!)

OPSWORKS TERMINOLOGY

 Some terms used in OpsWorks (a stack such as an application) may sound famil-IAR for you, but OpsWorks often puts your Twist on a term meaning. Here are the mini-dictionary of your terms:

Stack: A complete program that includes several tiers and cases, is a CON-sistent with CloudFormation terminology. Application-level elements, such as drawings (which are definitions of which software components are installed in a specific stack), users and AWS resources for each task (S3 bucksks and elastic loads Balancing devices, for example) are defined in a level stack.

Layer: A layer determines how to create and configure related versions and resources, such as EBS volumes. Most people may turn to class as an Applica-TION level – as a tier application, a class that performs one of the features of a definition in the context of an application. For example, a class can run a PHP environment to run a logical application. In order to reduce the burden of AWS service development, Amazon offers predefined numbers of configured layers –

such as Ruby, PHP, HAProxy (load Balancing), memcached, and MySQL – which you can use as or expand to meet your specific needs. These classes can be combined to form a full OpsWorks application.

Instance: the instance becomes a layer member and is configured to meet the needs of their work layer. The configuration includes setting the size and location of the availability zone for which it is running. The version can also be formed part of the automatic Zoom group in order to maintain a chaotic program workload.

Program: A specific code application that you write to perform the Func-ness you want to make. There are other parts of the OpsWorks that help you install and run the program code. To make your application code in the case of class, you have ADVAN-Tage and wonder which is the Chef. (In fact, OpsWorks uses the Chef to install his own neces-Sary software which it has before it revolves to install his application code.)

Monitoring, logging: Monitor the collection of COM-Plex versions, components and configurations that are part of the current application, OpsWorks install CloudWatch, implementation of advanced logging, as well as monitor environmental application, use open Code in the Ganglion tool.

What AWS management services should I choose?

The fact that Amazon offers three application management solutions is like proclaiming blessings and curses. The application solutions amazon provides indicate that many of its users have difficulty managing complex applications, but the availability of multiple solutions can make it more difficult to decide which solution to use.

Here are some guidelines for choosing a management solution to accept: If your application is very straightforward and written in a dynamic language, choose Elastic Beanstalek. If this database is very simple, I refer to an application running on a single tier that is not part of the application version, but you are using AWS RDS to manage persistent storage.

If your application is in a dynamic language, but you have written multiple levels of software, it is too complex for elastic beanstalek. Cloud formation is a good choice if your application is complex, but using images on Amazon computers that contain system resources (operating system and middleware (such as databases or other servers) and application code is a good choice. It can manage multiple layers and sublayers, even if they are autoscale. Cloud formation is not used to manage middleware and applications that are automatically installed in a single instance.

Of course, you need to be satisfied with the very complex JSON script so that you can use clouds that may or may not be your cup of tea. OpsWorks is a good choice if you use DevOps Lifetime Procedures, or if you want to automatically install code into an application version, or if you prefer JSON's graphical interface. You should be familiar with the chef because it is a code management method in the OpsWorks system. OpsWorks isn't in the long market (at least not when I wrote this book), but I'm looking forward to it. Become a common tool for managing complex application deployments.

10 REASONS WHY YOU SHOULD USE AMAZON WEB SERVICE

Many users of AWS are trying to explain why they start. Yet others are interested in AWS, but they don't exactly know what it is. And others know what is happening, and why they start it, but do not speak to justify their decision in leadership. To solve all these problems with a dirty swoop, here is a list of ten best reasons to use AWS.

1. AWS provides agility

It has its own reputation as "Department of No. "Although some institutes have enjoyed it with so-called intractness, where innumer and annotation obstacles are put on the way to search for any wizards. Infrastructure, "some of their respective networks and laws in order, many different resources have expressed sheer complexity by the fans, all of which should be vaccine with the production of computing resources. The result of the killing construction in the most system of this multishared mont, manual, attempt to collect time, which will result in a few months for a week in the distribution periods in order to free the Permanent Educational Fund of all this Conclusion: It is sluggish from Moldova and what it hates.

Amazon, as it is, it works from scratch and pondered its own management strategy as a base and is used as service. Because every part of the infrastructure is being held in the API, no human interaction is required for installation or resource configuration. However, because identifiers are provided in a fine grain manner (IP addresses are only derived from the storage, such as regular expressions), the resources can be defined and started in parallel, and it does not result in one step at a time Is. Results: Resources are available in minutes, weeks or months.

Aws Provides Business Agility

Guess what? For example, if you are a business unit in a company's sales or human resources, it's called "No Department."

Now, in the face of a slow-running organization, it's not just an adhesive, it's dangerous for your business. The risk applies the result of the nature of the change. In the past, it mainly referred to automated - in-house processing applications - payment volumes, invoicing, file management - usually as a recording system because they, uh, recorded information. Applications may now be used to communicate with customers, and, of course, to implement their needs - "self-service". These applications are often referred to as participatory C-levels because they facilitate engagement with parties outside the organization. And it will take time to meet customers' growing expectations for smartphones, tablets and the latest websites. When I felt I was using one company, I had an online way to check the status of my order, and I immediately looked forward to providing the same potential to other companies.

If they don't offer other companies, I'll probably find other suppliers as expected. In other words, to meet today's customers, businesses must quickly roll out new applications, in other words. AWS also supports more features. It is no secret that an important part of the AWS user base consists of business units that must adapt to AWS and its lengthy management processes. Adopting this business unit is sometimes called shadow, or, even more abominable, deceiving it.

Whatever you call it, it's time to make adjustments because business units feel the need to quickly aggregate new applications to respond to market demands and how long they respond to AWS business to help with more Tizen

Aws Provides A Rich Ecosystem Of Services

Another disadvantage of cloud service providers is how users build applications with features such as queues, managing alerts, and dynamic scanning (in response to user load).

Although these other services provide demanding virtual machines, the software is an exercise for students to build applications and components and external services (so to speak). Building an application can take a long time, so it can take a long time because devel is required to install and configure components of the cross-software. For components that require a commercial license, you must be able to arrange payments - this can take a long time, budget approval, and complexity of agreement negotiation. An online service, such as one, may not be available on a selected cloud service provider, so a call on the Internet requires access to the service in any other online location, which is called network privacy and outage.

Amazon offers a rich service environment that provides the benefits of your favorite search engines, so it's quick and less difficult:

A range of services as part of its AWS offerings: the full yability of building blocks that meet its service base, such as object and volume storage, and platform services such as queues and e-mail, such as flexibility and the extent to which the punching axis is rolled out to all paths. Many third-party companies host services on AWS: for example, both companies provide application integration services in centrifuges and Dell Marine AWS.

AWS users can merge applications running in AWS through services and will not exit AWS network traffic due to low network latency and improved application performance. All local (and most third-party) AWS services use the same pricing model as AWS: pricing is standard and easy to handle online.

As a result, users must avoid long-term negotiations and large upfront payments and tend to demand payments, which is consistent with AWS users. One of the rich AWS ecosystems is low triglycerides, but AWS is the most valuable aspect. Rapid response (in other words, agility) is often especially important for today's business.

Rich AWS environment systems increase agility, which is an important reason to use AWS.

AWS simplifies operations IT operations are endless and infinite. In fact, the term Sisyphean may be a term that was created to describe the timeless work of IT resource management. At the beginning of this chapter, I explained how AWS simplifies resource conditions, but AWS also facilitates the prosecution.

First, because the AWS is responsible for many of the traditional IT infrastructure, such as buildings, power supplies, networks and physical servers, it has a lot of work in the IT segment and load immediately reduced. IT operations. "But wait," as the information company says, "There's more!" In addition to being responsible for physical infrastructure, AWS has a significant IT management load associated with system operations. For example, the Relational Database Service (SDR) is responsible for running the database, backing up the database, and restarting instances that do not provide the required activity time.

All these tasks are important, taking the time and energy of people. By simplifying IT operations, AWS allows users to focus on what really matters in this area: applications.

In fact, AWS allows users to spend more of their IT budget on the qualities that differentiate their business while reducing their investment in important but undifferentiated tasks that are comparable to Keep the lights on AWS.

AWS is organized in different regions, and Amazon has regions around the world: several locations in the United States, Europe, South America and Asia Pacific. Because AWS is a global service, users can take advantage of nearby services to reduce network latency and improve application performance.

AWS's global capabilities also provide an ecosystem of local services in the form of local consulting services and system integrators, making it easy for users to get help in their native language and their local knowledge.

Amazon continues to roll out new regional locations, so you have access to nearby service locations and a rich AWS ecosystem.

AWS is one of the leading providers of cloud computing Services Hall of Fame baseball Catcher Yogi Berra is an intelligent typeface that is expressed in an apparently confusing way. Once, when he invited a popular restaurant, he politely refused, saying, "Nobody is there anymore - it's too crowded.

Today, Amazon has an intensive cycle that is produced:

Having more users generates more usage, which increases the amount of Amazon hardware purchases to reduce costs through economies of scale, which are delivered to users at lower prices.

Because of the large number of users, companies that provide integrated services, such as online application integration, decide to put their services in AWS, making the overall service better and therefore attracting more users . As more people and companies use AWS, more knowledge is available in the form of human capital and other resources (like this book!).

This knowledge makes AWS more attractive, making it easier for new users to start and increase productivity quickly. So, unlike Iogui, you should embrace the popularity of AWS and recognize that its position as the largest cloud service provider will bring you great benefits, and that these benefits will continue to grow as services Develop, It is another gift that is constantly given.

AWS Provides Innovation

Everywhere they turn, the word of innovation is a hot topic. People would realize that innovation makes life better and can improve the future of generation. It would probably not surprise you because of my excitement with AWS, knowing that I am firmly convinced that there is no Amazon presence in the cloud. Not all of the incumbent technological market leaders had an incentive to change the way they worked. It was necessary to go aside as Amazon, which was not a hereditary attempt to protect, thinking again in the way that technology was delivered.

AWS has changed the way technology is offered to customers, and as a result, it has enabled innovations to explode. Innovation and low cost associated with AWS enable small and large businesses to initiate new offers quickly and at cheap. As one innovation Consultant said: "AWS has reduced the price of failure. With AWS, you can easily experiment with new production to see if this is about "getting around ". Also, if the new offer is tighter and begins to accelerate, it can easily adjust it. On the other hand, if the service does not reach adoption, it is not a problem – the ease of the AWS resource shutdown means that there is not much loss if the potentially unis purchase is not interrupted. "

AWS IS COST EFFECTIVE

AWS is cost-effective, commentators who analyze the trends in Silicon Valley point out that the cost of starting an online store today is less than 10% of what was ten years ago.

The main reason for the cost reduction is AWS: it is cheaper on demand, easily terminating and without penalty, so you can use the compute capacity you need when you need it and pay it. However, the cost-effectiveness of AWS is not limited to start-ups. Each COM can benefit from access to inexpensive calculations that do not require lengthy promises.

This is a sign of the AWS force that many existing supply communities are afraid of what happens when customers start to put their prices and comfort. Amazon is a unique company. Unlike many companies that strive to improve their profitable margins, Amazon brings benefits of efficiency at a lower price.

There is no reason to expect this access to change. If you're part of any company or larger company, Amazon can further take IT space.

This is more cost-effective than the traditional model of access to IT resources: High pre-pay fees, little certainty, whether the amount is too small (or too large).

AWS aligns the organization with the future of technology.

Every 10 to 15 years, the IT industry is deeply disrupted by the incarnation of the new platform, a new form of computing that is changing the way applications are built and applied. The rise of threaded computers (customer server architecture) in 1980 transformed brilliance into an older environment and led Microsoft to become a dominant player in software industry.

Similarly, the Internet of the 1990s made the Web (and HTTP protocol) de facto architecture for all applications - and brought Domi-Nance companies like Google and, yes, Amazon.

Cloud computing is the next-generation computing platform. Its on-demand IT services, ordered by carp, highly scalable and available in minutes and which do not have a long-term appointment requirement, will become the basis of all future applications. As they say, their resistance is questionable.

Amazon Web Services, which are by far the leading industrial IT agent, are growing at a speed of more than 100 percent. Its record on innovation and price competitiveness is not comparable in this sector. I predict that in ten years AWS will be at a time when it will be Microsoft or Google. Your organization needs to familiarize itself with the AWS and understand how to use it effectively - otherwise it could be equivalent to the buggy manufacturer when Henry Ford invented the circuit.

AWS IS GOOD FOR YOU

A great quarry is built on the fact that the right person is in the right place at the right time. Being the right person is all about you - your ability to work hard, productive working relationship and intelligence. These controlled carp will help you succeed regardless of the field or role in which you work.

But to get to the right place, there is much in common with the observation where there is a new market that would allow some kind of innovation, and will be planted its flag. People who moved to the automotive industry in 1920, or the television industry of the 1950s or the Internet in the 1990s, faced huge opportunities, because the new market required expertise that would allow construction big business.

Technological innovations create major flaws in the industry, making knowledge and experience invaluable. If you believe AWS is the next-generation platform, it can also be the "right place at the right time" for you.

SEARCH ENGINE OPTIMIZING FOR AMAZON

The Amazon Associates program is an excellent affiliate program if you are an entrepreneur. You will have the opportunity to sell just about anything from dvds, to books, games and electronics. Some people focus on niche markets, while others choose to provide everything under the sun. Beginners can choose to add products to their sites by copying and pasting the code that Amazon provides. This is very simple to do and doesn't take any time to get started. Amazon makes it easy to be a partner. More advanced users may choose to utilize the amazon web services

No matter what method you choose to use, it will be important for you to get new users to your site. Part of getting new users to your site will be getting your product pages indexed into the search engines. You will want to practice traditional seo techniques such as adding keywords and page titles to your pages. In addition to optimizing your individual product pages, you will also want to manage a link campaign, with one way links pointing to your important category pages.

You will want to work on integrating the Amazon product information into your style or design so that while you might have similar text as other sites, overall it can be a totally different page from everything else on the net. Incorporate client testimonials, search boxes, feature products and menus in an innovative package, which will help you largely in providing value to your sites visitors and to the search engines as well.

Amazon Web Services will be the biggest challenge as you deal with large volumes of dynamic content. This doesn't have to be a problem as http://www.awswebshop.com has displayed. They've found a way to optimize their pages in a way that is attractive to their visitors and to the search engines. Each of their product pages have keywords and unique page titles, impressive.

Remember that Amazon offers millions of products, so, if you use the amazon web services, you open the door to having millions of pages indexed in the search engines. Think about that for a second, millions of pages equals millions of potential landing pages to your site. Even if you didn't sell anything which would be pretty hard to do (unless you didn't add a buy button), you've still got plenty of web real estate to put contextual ads on or other advertising.

Having a website that provides Amazon Web Services gives you the ability to have a recurring revenue stream so, there is lots of potential to have a long lasting cash flow. There isn't any cost to fee to join the Amazon Associates program, and because it's one of the oldest and known affiliate programs, you can find lots of documentation and even blogs about how to earn revenue.

As part of any seo strategy, you will want to add an rss feed and sitemap. Both will help with getting your pages indexed faster. Amazon does have copy and paste code available for the novice user to use, more advanced users will develop a custom feed of some sort. Once you have made search engine friendly changes to your site, can stand back and watch the crawlers come index your site.

AMAZON WEB SERVICES IMPORTANCE

Amazon's AWS offering has now become a huge operation compared to its launch way back in 2006... when I say huge, I mean huge. To give you an idea of scale, the comparable infrastructure and computing power that supported the entire AWS offering back in 2006 is now added each and every day to satisfy ever growing demand.

AWS is spread across eight geographic areas, with local edge locations to provide proxy caching nearest to your location. This provides both redundancy, high availability and improved performance.

AWS provides a fairly complete set of services to run almost anything you like and practically on a scale that is only really limited by how much you're willing to spend. This gives CIO's and CTO's options to play with but there is still some reticent about what should or should not 'go into the cloud'...

So what can it offer you? Well, helpfully AWS provide 'Reference Architectures' to help you conceptualize particular architecture scenarios. You can find approaches to help you with Large Scale Processing, Batch Processing, Disaster Recovery, Online Gaming and of course their bread and butter eCommerce approach.

Is it Secure?

Debates still rage over 'security in the cloud' and while cloud services are maturing it would be wrong to simply assume that the security aspect will somehow simply go away.

AWS is probably as secure as it can be, at least on paper. AWS will reassure you with Multi-Factor Authentication, Encryption and various security accreditation's up to military levels. You can even implement your own security models to your own standards. The question has to be answered, though, do you trust AWS to manage and protect your data and services? On the flip side given that AWS have 'handed over the keys' to the customer to build their own services security becomes a shared responsibility. For each customer the view, approach and even the decision will be different. Local laws may also effect your decision about what type of data you are allowed to host.

What Technology is Available?

The following are some of the key services and solutions on offer at AWS...

Compute Ec2 - This is the 'elastic compute' cloud virtual machine instances which can be 'rented' and configured by the characteristic of the workload from mobile phone to large scale cluster systems. Dedicated hardware is assigned for High Instance usage.

Cloud Watch monitoring - This service will auto-scale your environment based on performance monitoring and will add more instances as required based on demand. Transport for London use this service to scale their operations on demand.

Workspace - This is a fully managed desktop environment using the G2 graphics instance supporting desktop products like Windows on Nvidia GRID GK104 Kepler GPU's

Simple Storage - S3 is a highly scalable storage platform used by the likes of DropBox, Shazam and of course Amazon's retail business. Objects held within S3 are copied around the availability zones to reduce delays and improve caching.

Elastic Block Store - This provides persistent block level storage volumes for use with Amazon EC2 instances. Replicated across availability zones.

Glacier - Backup for long term archival. Pricing is based on number of requests (metered) Can take 3-5 hours to retrieve objects.

AWS Public Data Sets - These are free to use data sets hosted on a Hadoop platform they include data sets like: NASA NEX, Human Genome, Census Data and PubChem

Kinesis - Kinesis is a managed service that scales elastically for real-time processing of streaming big data and is used in conjunction with EC2 instances.

There's More?

In addition to these 'virtual' services, AWS can even provide dedicated physical connections such as dual 10gig lines into their data centres from your offices should you require it.

If you work in research then AWS can be useful from a grant point-of-view. You can now use a pre-pay solution where you can call off costs/credits as you go.

If you're a heavy user then AWS also allow you to 'bid' for services via their Spot Market. This is a pricing model targeted for batch processing and allows ad-hoc provisioning at a cheaper rate than normal provisioning costs.

For the average business though, you are more likely to choose a hybrid approach, where you choose to run your tightly coupled development in house and simply use AWS for everything else. The point is you have a choice, and AWS will almost certainly solve at least some of your challenges.

AMAZON WEB SERVICES FOR MANAGERS

When explaining AWS for the first time to managers (or anyone, for that matter) it is best to talk in concepts rather than in concrete terms. I've also noticed it is beneficial to try to tangiblize the discussion with familiar terms. Using terms like "Elastic IP" gets quizical looks, but calling it a publicly accessible IP address helps people to get a better overall grasp of concepts before using the AWS terms for things.

Hierarchical Organization

At a very high level, you can think of EC2 as a global computing environment. Within EC2 are geographical regions that can be thought of as data centers. Inside of these data centers are computer clusters that in AWS parlance are called Availability Zones:

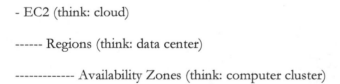

- EC2 (think: cloud)

------ Regions (think: data center)

------------- Availability Zones (think: computer cluster)

Virtual Machines

Inside of an Availability Zone, we have can create virtual machines from predefined or custom Amazon Machine Images, or AMIs. An AMI can be thought of as a snapshot of machine that you can load and run inside the cloud at an Availability Zone. Each time you take an AMI and start it, it is called an Instance of the AMI. You can take an AMI and start it several times, each time creates a new Instance.

Instances are virtual machines that are running, and I really mean they are virtual. If precautions are not taken, these virtual machines can wink out of existence and cause a great deal of consternation. So you don't really want to think of an Instance as something that is robust and persistent. It is merely a unit of computational resources.

Virtual Hard Drives

To help keep your data intact even when an Instance dies, you can use several different AWS services but one of the more common ones is the Elastic Block Store, or EBS. Think of EBS as a hard drive. You can make an EBS from 1GB to 1TB and 'install' it on any of your virtual machine Instances. So, if you have an Instance that is running your website and you want to make sure the database stays healthy even if the Instance disappears, you can use an EBS 'hard drive'. In the vernacular of AWS, you have created an EBS volume and mounted it on an Instance.

Other Virtual Storage

There are other services you could have used besides EBS for holding this imaginary database of yours. For example, the SimpleDB, or SDB, is a perfectly reasonable substitute and would be preferred in certain situations. However, SDB is a specific service for basic database delivery, whereas EBS is a generalized storage solution. There is also the Relational Database Service, or RDS that provide robust database services beyond SDB. The choice of service is often dependent upon the needs of the solution.

Virtual Backup

If we want to secure that data we now have on our EBS volume, we aren't out of the woods yet because even hard drives can fail. We'll want to back this up into more stable storage. For this we can use the Simple Storage Solution, or S3 for short. You can think of S3 as a readily available tape backup. It allows you to have up to 100 directories of data on your tape. Each of these directories is called a bucket in the S3 world. Because it is a good stable storage system, you will want to backup your EBS volume(s) to S3 periodically. And, if you have customized your Instance, you will want to save a new image of it in S3 also. This way, if your carefully customized Instance or EBS volume crashes for any reason, you can pull them out of your backup in S3 fairly quickly and get up and running again.

Robust Security

Well, all of this would be worthless if we didn't have good security to make sure our solution was hacked. Two concepts are used in AWS for security purposes. The first is a set of keys that allows you and your developers to gain access to your systems. These are public/private key pairs and digital certificates necessary to securely log into the Instance. The second, called a security group, can be thought of as a firewall configuration. You create a security group that defines how outside entities - such as web browsers, or remote desktops, or ftp, or email, etc. - can or cannot access your Instance.

Virtual Router

To serve our website to the public, we will need to have a permanent public IP address that we can assign to our Instance. For this we use an Elastic IP, or EIP. It is 'elastic' because although it is a fixed public IP on the Internet, it can be assigned to any of our Instances on the inside of AWS. This is a big plus because if that Instance dies and we bring up a new Instance, we can move the EIP to this new Instance and minimize site interruptions.

Cloud Scalability

Our site is up and running on our Instance, our data is safely on an EBS volume, we have backups on S3, well securely given our engineers access, and we have our site publicly accessible. All is well up to the point that we discover increased traffic from elsewhere in the world. Apparently, our site is popular in a geographical region that is distant from the region in which we set up our system. For example, we might have set up our website in the US, but we are getting 50% of our hits from Europe. Performance of our site for our European visitors will not be as good as we would like. Fortunately, we can push our site out closer to these users by using the Content Delivery Network, or CDN.

In AWS, CDN services are delivered by CloudFront. This service takes your static content and replicates closer to where you have a high volume of users, thereby making the delivery of your site much faster.

I hope this helps anyone interested in AWS and needs just a manager's overview of how it all works from a conceptual perspective. Please note that AWS is a constantly evolving system and new services and capabilities are added regularly.

AMAZON WEB SERVICES AND THE AMAZON USER

Applications can be easily layered with the help of flexible, reliable and cost-effective services provided by Amazon. Do you know the best part about Amazon Web Services? The fact that it is used as a platform-as-a-service is conducive to varied applications. You can pay as you go without any upfront expenditure. Additionally, since the hardware is taken care of by Amazon itself, you do not even have to pay any maintenance charges for the same.

The virtual infrastructure can be quickly set up while a similar real world setup would have taken a lot of time, sometimes weeks to create. Also, the infrastructure is quite flexible, elastic and scalable. Many companies opt for a virtual infrastructure since it becomes quite cumbersome and pricey to include a real-world solution, especially in the testing phase.

Virtual infrastructure also helps in creating innovative solutions and also helps in focusing on core business aspects. One does not need to worry about the number of servers to set up an infrastructure. Building and maintaining infrastructures usually takes about more than 70% of the time as per Amazon. AWS comes in the picture here, to save on the time involved to set up the infrastructure. The hardware and infrastructure is taken care of by Amazon and just makes it practically available for your use all the time. You just have to take care of your own tasks at hand and focus on innovative ideas to boost your business.

The Amazon Users Group promotes the activities involved with AWS which is also the world's largest provider of cloud computing services. The Amazon User Group is especially a forum for everybody to share their experiences about cloud computing. If anybody is interested in learning more about Amazon and its various services and also about how profitable it is to use AWS in your organization, then the group can help out the users.

One can even address queries related to the technical aspects of AWS cloud computing platform and also explore the different ideas and concepts which can be combined into business opportunities unrestricted by the use of hardware resources.

AWS has boosted the growth of cloud computing to a great extent and is an accessible way to access cloud computing. One can discuss in the Amazon User group about the evolving approaches related to software application development, system management, capacity scaling and other topics. There are more than existing plan-of-actions which can be tapped for using AWS and its services.

AMAZON WEB SERVICES - LOWER STARTUP COSTS

When starting up a new online service, companies can find many advantages when utilizing some of Amazon's AWS platforms. As an experienced developer, I have used several of these services and can recommend them to other people starting online services or dynamic websites.

Amazon Web Services (AWS) began in 2002, leveraging the infrastructure already in place by one of the internet's largest e-tailers. AWS provides a range of web services which can form what is now becoming popularly known as a "cloud".

Currently on offer by AWS are approximately 20 web services to be used in the cloud. The most popular to date are the Elastic Cloud Compute and Simple Storage Service, respectively known as EC2 an S3.

S3

Perhaps the service which existing website owners can take advantage of the quickest, is Amazon's Simple Storage Service (S3). S3 is an online file storage system with built-in high redundancy and infinite scalability. Amazon uses clusters of servers across the globe to guarantee up to 99.999999999% retention and 99.99% up-time to any data you upload to S3.

Any existing files (up to 5GB in size per file) from a website can be easily migrated to S3, allowing it to be used as a Content Delivery Network (CDN). Amazon's AWS infrastructure resides on super fast internet backbones, which means content will generally be served much faster than if it were served from cheap shared hosting accounts. For the relatively cheap price per GB of storage and data transfer, many website owners currently using web hosting with limited storage and bandwidth may see instant cost reductions by migrating to S3 for content delivery.

For large websites and online services which serve massive amounts of data, the cost performance of Amazon's S3 can be very high and in some cases a necessary tool when other services cannot store such large amounts of data.

For a company considering starting up an online file sharing or content-heavy service such as a photo or video sharing site, Amazon S3 offers many benefits and a performance which would otherwise require a large initial cost outlay.

EC2

Amazon's Elastic Cloud Compute (EC2) is for server hosting what S3 is for file storage - infinitely scalable and cost effective.

With EC2, you can setup your own cluster of virtual servers running in Amazon's cloud of servers. You may choose to run a single, low-power virtual server or a cluster of thousands of high performance virtual servers, and any variation in between. Each server you run is called an "instance" and you may choose to use an instance for as little as one billable hour.

Being able to choose how long you use an instance, along with how powerful it is, allows start-up companies to test a new powerful web application without the need to provision costly hardware initially. This alleviates a lot of the risk often encountered with web start-ups who must calculate how much capacity they will need once the site becomes popular. Under-estimating capacity can mean a disruption of service, over-estimating will make the service less profitable.

The EC2 platform is totally programmable, too, which means companies can build intelligent systems which will scale as capacity limits per instance are encountered. When the server load is high, for example, more instances can be turned on and share the load of the system. When the load decreases, unneeded instances can be powered down, keeping costs and efficiency steady.

Currently, there are various Windows and Linux Amazon Machine Instances (AMIs) available for users to use as a starting point when customizing their virtual servers. User-contributed AMIs are also available, with purpose-built server configurations available.

Pairing EC2 & S3

For new startups and existing web services looking to migrate, a combination of EC2 server hosting and S3 as a Content Delivery Network can be an ideal solution. For those able to use both services, there is an added benefit in that inter-network traffic between your EC2 and S3 accounts will usually be free of any bandwidth costs.

EC2 MICRO INSTANCES

Micro instance (t1.micro) type is one of the most fashionable and highly acceptable instance types by IT fellows supported by Amazon EC2. During November 2010, AWS announced the free tier and started offering 750 hours of Micro Instance usage free per month for the first one year, but it's available as an Amazon EBS-backed instance only. You can now launch EC2 within a Virtual Private Cloud (VPC). AWS now extends to t1.micro instances running inside of a VPC also.

Talking to it technical specifications, the Micro Instance type doesn't have that much power required for heavy stimulating. The main memory presented in Micro instance type is 613MB. It comes with explode CPU capacity that can be goes up to 2 Elastic Compute Units (ECU). That means the CPU performance is not conventional. This is just not enough for running any severe workloads. And yes, storage can be added through Elastic Block Storage (EBS) and the free tier covers up to 30GB of storage space.

Best Recommendation when optimizing an AMI for the micro instance type:

• Design the AMI can run on at max. 600 MB of Memory Usage

• Edge the number of chronic processes that use CPU time (e.g., cron jobs, daemons)

But from the technical specification it doesn't mean Micro Instances are totally ineffective. They offer excellent worth in certain cases. In this article, I want to share how to get the best out of the Amazon EC2 MI.

Optimize Swap Memory - This is pertinent to Linux based Micro Instances. By default, these types of instances do not have swap space configured at initial level. I ran my Cloud Magic World Website on a MI for a few days. During the crest loads, I have experienced Apache Server or MySQL crashing unexpectedly. So with just 613 MB at your clearance, you got to make sure that you have set aside enough disk space for the swap.

Auto Scaling Out - The funda on the Cloud is auto scaling out. Running a convoy of low-end servers in parallel is more competent and cost effectual on any virtualized infrastructure. As per the load and use-case, splitting a job across number of Micro Instances may be cheaper and faster than running the same job on a single Large Instance. This scale out structural design provides better fail over and quicker processing.

Mull over Caching - If you are scheduling to host sites on these, be clear in your mind that they are not very dynamic. Dynamic websites demand more CPU power and memory due to the approach each request is processed. Straightforward websites like blogs and marketing sites with a few dynamic contents are ideal participants for the Micro Instances. Moreover, consider caching the content to avoid CPU spikes. For example, if you are running any blog or website, you can enable caching plug-ins to increase the performance. There are plenty of plug-ins available for caching by free of cost.

Select 64-bit - Always pick 64-bit when running it. This is assured to give you better recital than the 32-bit complement. You will see the difference when you are running batch processing that deals with large files and processes.

Pull the Cron jobs - Many patrons operate a Linux Micro Instance to run cron jobs and precise locale tasks that monitor and handle their entire AWS infrastructure. If you want to run a cron job, stop all other running services, add swap space to instance and pull it to make it a tilt and mean cron job machine.

MAKING MONEY WITH AMAZON STORE SERVICES

When is the last time you used Amazon.com to buy a product? I'm sure it was only a few weeks, day or even hours ago. As great as Amazon is for buying products and services online, their business and web site is also a great source for making money online and generating revenue through the use of their web site and associates program. Let's take a deeper look into the Amazon business and how you can start making money with their web site.

- Selling on Amazon

Did you know you can sell your own products through the Amazon web site? Sell products and gain exposure to the tens of millions of shoppers who are using Amazon.com every day. There are also no per-item listing fees.

- Amazon Web Store

If you are familiar at all with eBay, then you may already understand the concept of buying and selling products online. Through Amazon you can also setup your own branded high power and fully functioning e-commerce web site. Using the same technology Amazon uses to run their web site, you can have an online store up and running in no time.

- Fulfillment by Amazon

Shipping and processing not letting you take your business to the next level? Amazon.com also offers fulfillment services where they can pickup and ship products for you.

- Checkout by Amazon

It seems like everyone is trying to get into the credit card processing game and Amazon is no exception. Through the use of Amazon's check out system you can start accepting orders online through your own online store.

- Amazon Advantage

As technology continues to progress, so does the need for the way we buy and sell products. Instead of buying a movie at the store, download it online instead. Using Amazon Advantage, you can utilize the self service consignment program to sell media products directly on Amazon.com.

- Amazon Associates Program

If you have a web site or know how to setup online ad campaigns, you can make money using the Amazon Associates program. You will earn a commission on every referred lead sent to that results in a new sale. Through the use of their associate program, you do not have to process any orders or hold any inventory. Associates of Amazon have earned hundreds of millions of dollars over the years.

As you can see, there are many ways that you can start earning revenue and generating sales through the use of Amazon.com. No matter how your business works, there is a different solution for you.

GETTING PUBLISHED WITH AMAZON PUBLISHING

If your goal was to become a famous author who went on speaking engagements and book signings in between fabulous vacations, reality may have hit you hard at some point in your career. Amazon publishing is doing something about that roadblock now. The print on demand and e-book market is exploding in popularity.

This increase in attention to web based publishing is causing the big six mega publishers stand up and take notice. Both Apple and Google have entered the fray with the universal tools (iBook) and the content (Google books). Amazon has no interest in being left out of this market considering that they are still the leader in online book sales. They are empowering the small publisher to get their works out in easier market penetration and production. Since their wildly popular eBook reader (Kindle) appeared in 2007, electronic book sales have overtaken print in numbers.

What will it take to get your dream project in print or on screen in front of millions? If you've done the work and have your project ready, there are still a few crucial steps that you'll need to take.

This part could be more troublesome that actually getting your book out. That's because there are many steps in the production and distribution process to attend to prior to printing (in the case of print on demand) and even electronic format for the Kindle. Once you know all the steps that Amazon needs to qualify the material for publication, you're ready.

These steps are crucial to getting paid and being noticed as well as producing the kind of product that will have Amazon wanting you to get moving on another project because your first one made them money. That is the key to the relationship with this book-selling giant. If you please their bottom line, they will bend over backward to please you.

The steps get easier with the help of experts who have had a history of working with Amazon successfully. They can show you how to work with the company so that you get the most favorable result for your business. They understand that there is always money left on the table when a mega-giant is calling the shots.

Amazon will provide templates and guidelines for your book; they will also penalize you messing it up. That is why it is in your best interest to find someone who knows the ins and out of working with his or her system. You'll want to know what book cover design works best for your market and how to maximize the promotional power of a "blurb". These are just a few of the areas to consider when you get started.

Amazon publishing services is a great vehicle for getting you into the spotlight and now that they are making the journey easier, you might end up in front of that audience after all. Be sure to consider the amount of effort needed to get your project in the hands of potential buyers.

IMPORTANCE OF WEB SERVICES FOR YOUR BUSINESS

The description of web services can be a very technical one, full of references to terms only computer technologists can understand. So just what are they? What happens if you use them? How will it help you and your business? Hopefully as you read this brief article you will gain a better understanding of the topic. When you employ someone to do these services for you, you will get custom designs tailor made to your needs; or a template on your computer could be copied for a fast, easy page. Web services are also known as application services. eBay and Amazon are two of the best known examples of these services in action.

A short but precise definition of web services is the following; interaction of at least two separate operations integrating through a system of connections to transmit information simultaneously. The operations interact, not the people using them. So, these services would enable a customer or just someone browsing the internet to use your site. This is just the tip of the iceberg, because the variety of applications that can be used is extensive. Say you own a website, for instance. You want to use the best applications on your site. Yet, you will want them to be simple to operate. You want to encourage the user to stay and come again to your site.

A computer graphic artist can help you at this point with web services that may consist of a logo, or just visually exciting interfaces for your site. Your site is a representation of you on the web. You will want the essence of your company to shine through your site. An artist is adept at using design and color to capture visually what you desire on your web page. Many programs are available nowadays that make the most of art and technology, for instance, Flash designs.

Maybe you have an older site that could use a fresh look. These services are also perfect for this type of thing. They can update your site to bring more traffic and sales to your online business. These services can also periodically perform maintenance on your site to make sure it is running efficiently and optimally. Web services additionally utilize SEO (search engine optimization) for maximum exposure of your site on the World Wide Web. Web content writers are additionally used to write content that will interest, inform, or otherwise attract users and customers to your site. Ultimately, these services are the catalyst providing the transformation of the internet.

TACTICS ON DISCOVERING THE AMAZON WEB SITE

The official site of Amazon.com, Inc. became operational i.e. went online in 1995. In just under two decades, the site has become the biggest online dealer and retailer of almost every type of product or service that covers almost all categories you can think of. You name it, they have it including products and services but not limited to consumer electronics, retail items, digital applications and contents, customized and branded labels, cloud computing, content production, donations and charities. Amazon started online retailing with books.

If you're thinking of launching your own start-up or want to take your existing business to the next level by going online, then Amazon's own success story will really work as a morale booster. It was once an innocuous start-up and now it is providing a platform to countless others to get started up. You too can join the bandwagon of those who have already used the amazon platform for promoting their business online and countless others who are registered online members of the Amazon online club. Take stock of the following six strategies on how best you can exploit the portal of Amazon for your business gains: -

1. Promote your products or services on Amazon.com: - Although Amazon is the largest online stocker of all sorts of products and services; it will stand you in good stead if you start with just a single product or service hitching on their 'sell on Amazon' plan. Thereafter, you can graduate to becoming a small merchant seller selling more than 10 items. You will be required to pay either a proportion or a flat amount per sale apart from a fixed fee every month. In return you'll get the benefit of using administrative, creative and technical tools to help increase your revenues.

2. Use the Amazon platform as an advertisement platform: - You can use the site for listing images of your product with lucid product details and' how to... ' instructions. This mode of promotion is much cheaper than using the 'selling on Amazon' program as you pay on pay-per-click (PPC) basis. Using the advertisement programs also involving furnishing minimum of details as far as your product or service is concerned. You at least don't have to keep uploading price lists, inventory lists and other details.

3. You can make your online store a sort of store within a large store: - Amazon offers you the opportunity of opening a 'webstore' if you are a greenhorn and hence inexperienced in online marketing. It's your own virtual store.

4. Use the fulfillment policy of Amazon to the hilt: -The best thing about promoting and selling through Amazon is that they undertake full responsibility of delivering your products safely to your customers, dealing with returns, and providing customer support.

5. Capitalize from Amazon's data storage and cloud computing services: - Apart from using Amazon's portal as an advertisement and selling platform you can make good use of web facilities for storing your files or valuable business data.

6. Use checkout by Amazon: - Irrespective of the online platform you're using to promote your products or services, you can always proffer 'checkout by Amazon' as a payment alternative to your customers.

AMAZON EC2 INSTANCE TUTORIAL

Creating an Amazon EC2 instance is incredibly easy as I will show you in this tutorial.

You will require the some things to get started:

1) A verified AWS account

Create your account with Amazon Web Services. Go to aws.amazon.com and set up an Amazon Web Services account. You should have a credit card and a phone number for pin validation. Note you could very well be eligible for a cost free micro instance for one year. You could use this for what we are setting up here, but be aware that you will still need to have a credit card to start the account. This will take a few minutes to get your account online right after you sign up. Get some espresso now if you desire.

If you have an email advising you that your account is set, we can now go in and create a server instance. Head back to the Amazon web services page and from the main menu, choose "AWS Management Console". If you want to set up the free usage tier - just stay within the limitations of the terms of service (mostly 1 micro instance) and you'll be good - you won't be billed for your first year.

So to start up an instance - select EC2 on the AWS Management Console. You'll be shown the EC2 console.

Click on the "Launch Instance" button.

Select the "Classic Wizard". You will be asked to choose an AMI. Now we will click on our instance. For this tutorial we'll use Ubuntu so decide upon either the Ubuntu Server 12.04 LTS or the Ubuntu Server 11.10 (I decided on the 12.04 LTS but each of them are fine for serving a website). I also decided on 64bit.

Instance Details

You will see on the next screen - we'll just select 1 instance. Verify the instance type is Micro and pick and choose "Continue". I just simply use the defaults for the kernel and RAM Disk ID settings.

Key Pairs

You will be prompted to setup a Key Pair. I left the Key set to the default of "Name" and for the Value - I used "Website" - this can be whatever you want. Essentially this names your instance so you could tell them apart if you have more than one. This can be edited later as well, but insert something in there in the meantime. Next, input a name for your key pair - this is necessary, but label it something readable like "ws", "website" or something you can remember. When you setup the key pair, a file will save to your desktop. Keep this safe and don't loose it. You will have to have it to connect to the server. Regarding security group settings, you may possibly leave them with the quick-start-1 defaults. Now you'll see a confirmation screen. You can go ahead and begin with the instance set up. This can take a few minutes. Play with the "refresh" button back on the console to assess the set up status.

Once you "refresh" you ought to see "1 Running Instance" on the "My Resources tab. This brings up the Instances list.

Select your instance and you will get the "details" panel beneath.

Basically from here you can see the data around the server instance. The relevant thing here is the Public DNS. It's the long URL - something like its ec2-34.235.33.21.compute-1.amazonaws.com.

So in this case, we have efficiently set up a server instance. The incredible thing about Amazon is these instances can be kicked off or terminated and you'll only pay for what you use. I had some mistakes when I first tried setting mine up - I made the decision later to change from Apache to Ubuntu. Not conscious what I was doing - I had generated 4 instances. You get invoiced by the hour so I terminated them. Total charge - 8 cents.

Ted Forbes is a photographer, writer, filmmaker and media producer from Dallas, TX. He maintains a blog on technology topics including an amazon ec2 tutorial. He's been a guest speaker at several major international conferences and spends most of his time teaching and working on new projects.

AMAZON'S SECRET PLAN

Where can you buy books, music, movies and the infrastructure to build the next MySpace, Flickr or YouTube?

Amazon.com has the worlds biggest retail site. That takes quite a bit of infrastructure to run a site like that...right? But an infrastructure like that is also a valuable commodity if you can monetize it...Amazon seems to be trying to do just that. They want to provide the infrastructure that will power the next wave of web sites. The amazing part of the Amazon Web Services offering is that there are no setup charges or other up-front costs required to setup a world-class scalable web application. If you can imagine it, you can build it...on the Amazon framework.

So here is what they are actually offering and what it means.

Amazon's Simple Storage Service (S3)

This is the gem of Amazon's web service offerings. Unlimited (theoretically) storage on tap. While there were some hiccups in the beginning and there are some limitations (5GB maximum object size), S3 provides scalable, highly available, secure persistent storage. I looked at this when it was first offered and while it was a beautiful service, it was hard to roll into certain types of products since control over the "secret" key needed to store objects was critical to security. It required certain back-flips to use a client installed package that could store objects to a central storage facility and pushing the data through a 3rd party web-host effectively limited the benefits of the famous S3 scalability.

Amazon's Elastic Computing Cloud (EC2)

This is so cool it's hard to fully describe. Think virtualization on steroids. Unlimited computing power on tap. No setup fee and a fee of 10 cents per processor hour and you've got something very interesting. It is a very technical service requiring quite a bit of knowledge and ability to setup but this just creates another market for technical shops to be able to offer support services for EC2 and the other services.

Amazon's Simple DB

Ok. By this time, if you have the next killer application in mind and all you need is some VC money to make it happen, you are starting to get excited. You are starting to see a strategy that will allow you to boot-strap your business and your application without shelling out the big bucks for the rack servers and the data center. Amazon's SimpleDB...one of the key elements that can pull it all together is exactly what it's name says it is. A simple database. But...a simple database that scales to extremely large numbers of connections, large numbers of tables and massive record counts. If you don't understand what that means for your application just think of it like this. You could build...well, the next Amazon.com on this platform.

Let's see...store the content on S3, put the data in SimpleDB and analyze the data for recommendations and other batch jobs using EC2. Wait a minute...this is really getting good.

Now, remember that I mentioned there was a problem with S3 with the secret key?

The problem was partly a security problem and partly a billing problem. S3 is billed on transfer and storage space. Not very much, but as you pack on the gigabytes, the pennies add up. So you either have to over bill to give you some room for customers who use more resources and make your profit on the backs of the customers who don't abuse the service, or you have to come up with some way of tracking usage. This is a tough thing to do and still retain scalability. Also, there is still the security issue. You have to really work to protect the secret key used to store your data. But...Amazon, either realized this and rushed filled the gap or always understood this and just didn't release the solution until recently.

Amazon's DevPay

DevPay is a commerce layer on top of S3 and EC2. Takes care of the security problem. Takes care of the billing problem. The only minor drawback is that the customer is a shared customer with Amazon even though you provide the application. For most applications this won't be a problem and if you built your app on S3, EC2 and SimpleDB anyway, well...you are already in bed with Amazon so this is not a tough pill to swallow.

The Other Stuff

Ok...there are other web services as well. There is SQS (Simple Queue Service), the Mechanical Turk (this one is really strange...you pay pennies for human power to perform repeatable, tedious tasks), the Flexible Payment Service (another commerce model that allows you to charge for services and goods using Amazon's commerce backend) and of course, Amazon's affiliate web services.

The thing about all this is that its not obvious. These web services have been rolled out quietly and the average person has no clue what this actually means. But there are quite a few businesses that are not only successfully using these services to launch their businesses, they are doing it with much larger profit margins and significantly less capital drain as a result.

They keep up like this and one day, there will be a handful of major players (especially if Microsoft succeeds with their hostile takeover of Yahoo) and a large number of medium and small web application/service providers with a large number of them using Amazon's platform.

Ok...now for my psychic act.

If Amazon does this well and proves the market (I have to admit, they seem to be doing it) , then Google will wake up and do the same thing and become the second major virtual application platform. Microsoft will realize that they missed the boat and quickly build their own boat on a .NET based platform and jump in.

The result with be good for all of us. New more powerful, more scalable applications running on AmazonSpace, GoogleSpace or .NETSpace with more features and lower operational costs.

MONEYMAKING IN AMAZON

There are many amenities that Amazon has to offer for buyers and sellers alike. But, the best way to benefit from the online retail website Amazon.com is through being a member and by knowing the different ways you can make money out of Amazon.

The first and most obvious reason is that you have the goods and they can help you sell it on Amazon itself. But what if you have your own website? Then, you too can have that head start with your e-business by using Amazon's 1-Click Ordering.

Also, through Amazon's product ads, a cost-per-click program that showcases your products to the millions of online shoppers, it's as simple as uploading your products and putting their price and voila! It's for the world to see! This program on requires minimal costs, allows you to gain more traffic on your site, and increases your chances of higher revenue, with more hits and clicks.

If your business is more service-oriented than that of your products, there is also the feature of Clickriver Ads, a site which also offers the team-up of your services being promoted alongside your products.

Another way to be able to maximize making money in Amazon is though its Fulfillment by Amazon (FBA) program. Through this, you get to store your products on Amazon's fulfillment centers, and they can safely and directly pack and ship those products, and offer quality customer service, on your behalf.

As a seller, no other site can guarantee the accuracy of your payments but through Checkout by Amazon, Amazon Simple Pay and Amazon Flexible

Payments, these programs ensure and have proven fraud detection and allow your customers to be able to access the most secure and trusted online payment solutions.

Amazon has so much to offer for everyone of different backgrounds whether you are an author, you can also avail of CreateSpace, a member of the Amazon group of companies, that provides a fast, easy and economical way to self-publish and share your content with potential customers on Amazon.com and other sites.

As a developer you can increase your site's productivity by the numerous programs that are offered such as Amazon WebStore, Marketplace Web Services, Fulfillment Web Services, Amazon Web Services, Advertising Web Services (Product Advertising API), Amazon Flexible Payments and Mechanical Turk.

All these affiliate programs, are in a solitary effort of making your e-commerce more up to date, and customer friendly, and allow developers to create newer and more innovative ways of handling the business, at the click of a button. They include all the tools needed to freshen up your site, up to the ways where payment can be made easier and more accessible.

WEB 2.0 MASHUP

The term Web 2.0 is all the rage, but it really doesn't provide much detail on what it really is. The Internet and associated web pages are in a constant state of evolution. The term Rich Internet Application (RIA) refers to a web page or application that provides the user with an experience that resembles applications running on their local computer. RIA is one aspect of the Web 2.0 evolution.

Another Web 2.0 example is something called a "Mashup". A mashup is a quick way of describing a web page or site that brings together information from multiple sources in a unique way that brings value to the web user. There are many examples of mashups out there. Perhaps the best examples are ones that display information on a map. Thanks to Google Maps and Microsoft Maps it has become easy to not only display a map but also display push-pins for specific locations along with interesting information about the locations. Think about trying to find a restaurant for dinner. Just enter in your desired area and a map can be displayed with push-pins showing possibilities and when you move your mouse to the push-pin the page displays information about the restaurant. Pretty cool and helpful for the user.

Not all mashups are created equal, and not all require the use of maps. In some cases the information that is displayed from the user is retrieved from multiple sources through the use of Web Services or other APIs. The use of web services or APIs typically requires some amount of programming knowledge or experience. I have created several mashups by combining the Amazon Web Services, eBay web services, and PriceRunner services to provide a valuable source of information to consumers.

Where to Start?

Create your own mashup is a great way to better understand what a mashup is. Where to start, however, depends on your level of technical skills. If you have some programming and web development skills, then the best place to start will be the web site ProgrammableWeb.com. That site has tons of information about mashups, published APIs from vendors and other web sites, examples of mashups, forums, and more. Even if you aren't interested in programming the site will provide you with some good information.

TECHNICAL BENEFITS OF AMAZON S3

A reliable data storage infrastructure for developers is Amazon simple storage service. This initial publicly available web service was launched in United States in March 2006 and in Europe in November 2007. About 102 billion objects is said to be stored in Amazons3 as the month of March 2010.This new service maximizes the benefits of scale and pass those benefits on to the developers. The present availability of this website is limited to US Standard, EU (Ireland), US West (Northern California) and Asia-Pacific (Singapore) Regions. The services provided by this website are really appreciable.You can earn money by publishing your book in this site. People choose this website when they want to buy books.

*It provides unlimited storage for your objects. Each object is stored in a bucket (each of which is owned by Amazon Web Services) and with the help of a developer-assigned key it is retrieved.

*The security of the data is ensured with help of an authentication mechanism.

*The specificity you give to your object region for storage is never changed unless you manually change it.

*REST and SOAP interfaces are used for AmazonS3.

*Protocols and functional layers updated at the time of your choice makes this application more flexible.

*It ensures the durability of your stored objects with a new mechanism of RRS (Reduced Redundancy Storage)

*AWS Management Console enables easy accession and management of your resources.

*Large amount of data transfer is accelerated with the help of AWS Import/Export.

*Provide highly durable storage for Web applications and also media files.

AMAZON PRIME AIR

When Amazon was launched, it began as a online bookstore. Outside the span of economic opportunity was the chance of enhancing the buyer experience by widening the customers' choice. Creating the world's first online bookstore was recognizing that, in 1995, you couldn't walk into any bookstore in the world and be able to review or purchase the millions of books in circulation. Even from the beginning, Amazon was focused on creating the best customer experience with a deliberate focus on convenience and the vision of pioneering other technological advancements as the end of the 21st century approached.

I believe it's fair to say that Jeff Bezos and many others, including myself, believed the 21st century would include the convenience of flying cars, the convenience of getting your annual checkup without having to visit the doctor's office, or being able to order a ride to anywhere in your city all at the press of a button. In 1995, all of these technological advances were just storylines of The Jetsons and other science fiction. Innovation has now made all but one of those storylines a reality - but I'm sure Elon Musk is working on getting us those flying cars.

Amazon has pioneered a number of technological innovations through their now-extensive product lines. From its conception, the company was focused on making every book available for purchase online, but their focus has now evolved into "selling everything to everyone." Over the last 16 years they have come closer and closer to that goal. Their product lines include:

Amazon Fresh (currently in beta), where they sell fresh produce.

Amazon Prime, which provides video and music content instantly to customers via their smart devices.

Amazon Fashion, which launched last fall.

Amazon Fulfillment.

Amazon Marketplace, which provides customers with the opportunity to become entrepreneurs while utilizing the company's logistics and distribution infrastructure.

Amazon Kindle, which I believe was the predecessor of all other tablet devices.

Amazon Web Services, which was a business born out of Amazon's necessity to create a sustainable infrastructure for their online operations. They did it so efficiently that they had extra capacity to support the infrastructure of other companies, some of which could be considered their competitors.

Their latest and possibly most ambitious endeavor, Amazon Prime Air, will revolutionize ecommerce as well as logistics and distribution. Amazon Prime Air extends the products that the company can sell. With a vision of leading innovation in Unmanned Aerial Vehicle (UAV) delivery, Amazon Prime Air will enhance all of their other product lines by allowing their customers to get the goods they order much faster, effectively enhancing the Amazon customer experience. Skeptics (including myself) have wondered how big is the customer base that would use such a service and why would anyone ask for a drone to come anywhere near their house. Drones definitely get a bad rap, and rightfully so, but most of those concerns are out of place within the APA discussion as these UAVs will not have missiles or cameras attached to them. So the real question is, does this product line and technology have a customer base or serve any real need outside of its "coolness" factor? Well, let's take a look at what the data says:

Amazon has been working on UAV technology for some time but it wasn't until November of last year that the Federal Aviation Association (FAA) announced a plan to create a standard for the commercial use of Unmanned Aircraft Systems (UAS). It is obvious that Amazon has to go on a public relations blitz to inject the acronym "U.A.V." into the public discourse in the place of "drone" in regards to APA as it will enhance the public's perception once they launch the platform. And according to the FAA's UAS commercial integration plan, they have plenty of time.

Here is the FAA UAS integration timeline. It is broken into 3 phases:

The first phase, Accommodation, extends into 2015. During this time, I believe Amazon will work to attain the Certificate of Airworthiness (COA). The second phase, Integration, extends into 2020, and in this phase I believe Amazon will mostly focus on beta testing in select markets. The third and final phase, Evolution, extends past 2021; Amazon would have not only developed a UAV ready to interact with the public but also a UAS that incorporates the various aspects of storage, fulfillment and distribution. At this point, they can expect that there will be many competitors who would also utilize UAVs as a form of logistics such as Fedex, UPS, other online retailers, and big box stores such as Walmart and Target. So Amazon's main focus at this point should be creating a UAV/UAS that will be the safest and most reliable, and not only meet FAA standards but exceed them with the goal of Amazon Prime Air becoming synonymous with UAV delivery. The FAA has made it clear that it is not a matter of if but when, and if Amazon follows through with its plan, it could pioneer a completely new form of delivery.

Google Trends

The day after Amazon Prime Air was announced on the show 60 Minutes happened to be the largest consumer holiday of the year, "Cyber Monday." It was also the first time that Cyber Monday surpassed Black Friday in sales. Utilizing the Google Trends tool I was able to gauge consumer interest. Google Trends is a research tool that allows users to gain insight on Google search data by comparing search phrases. In this graph "Cyber Monday" was at 100pts with "Amazon Prime Air" and "Amazon drone" representing 75 and 74 points respectively. So for every 4 people that searched for Cyber Monday deals, 3 searched for Amazon Prime Air. I believe it is fair to say that for every 4 people who made a purchase on Cyber Monday, 3 would have been a customer of Amazon Prime Air!

The data shows that there is some consumer interest, but whether this is a true reflection of real opportunity is to be confirmed. Regardless, a showing of 3 out of 4 consumers definitely leans towards further investigation. The opportunity and economics of this new business line must be examined. Amazon Prime Air's current prototype has a max payload of 5 lbs or less, which qualifies 86% of their shipments as eligible for Amazon Prime Air. According to resources, their free shipping policy on select orders cost the company about $6 billion just last year and with FedEx and UPS (their shipping partners) increasing the rate by 4.5% they can anticipate that this cost will go up and continue to increase over time. The data available on the Amazon Prime Air R&D budget is not publicly available so I had to get creative and also make a few assumptions. I deduced the opportunity cost by multiplying 86% of their daily shipping count which at its peak represents 13.5MM by the lowest 'one-day shipping' rate which is the closest service to Amazon Prime Air and then the highest 'one day shipping rate' and captured an amount totaling $52-103 billion. I then took this a step further, considering Amazon's customer-centric philosophy and their current business model of low margins. Even at a 2% margin they would still net $1-2 billion dollars. The opportunity is large enough that Amazon will either be a huge customer of UAV delivery or a huge provider of UAV delivery.

So far I've covered the vision, strategy, and the why (albeit briefly), and now for the execution of the most innovative product of the 21st century - so innovative that the government is still trying to determine the regulations.

Amazon Prime Air is the name of Amazon's unmanned aircraft system. The system will be developed by framing every possible user story with the consideration of their customers, the public, their employees at the fulfillment centers, the deployment, the UAV hub and most importantly, the unmanned aircraft vehicle.

At their current capacity of 96 fulfillment centers around the world, they do not meet the 10-mile distance requirement for the UAV prototypes, so as part of their strategy they would need to continue the development of fulfillment centers as part of the unmanned aircraft system.

UAV MVP

Amazon's primary focus should be creating a safe UAV, so discussing and developing user stories with the engineering team will be prioritized by safety, security, and reliability. They should also focus on defining and exploring specs utilizing current FAA requirements such as sense and avoid, control and communications and the others as detailed.

The current roadmap details the definition and exploration to meet FAA requirements within the next two months, exploring SAA technologies such as electro-optic, infrared, and radar, with the second phase focusing on building and testing of the UAV through the rest of the year. The last phase, focusing on developing the rest of the Amazon Prime Air system, will extend into 2015 calendar year.

Launching Amazon Prime Air will not be an easy task, as can be expected for such an ambitious endeavor, but I believe even with this brief analysis of the project, Amazon could lead in the innovation of UAV delivery.

MAKING YOUR AMAZON S3 INTO MORE THAN A SIMPLE STORAGE SOLUTION

Amazon S3 does what it says on the tin - provides a Simple Storage Solution!

The facility is increasingly popular for hosting images (including adverts), videos and music for users who enjoy this easy to use, scalable on demand, affordable storage solution. The most recent figures announced by Amazon's own Jeff Barr show an amazing 762 billion objects being stored on the facility representing annual growth of 290%.

S3 is much more than just a simple storage solution. S3 can generate log files and by analyzing these users have the opportunity to obtain a comprehensive real-time insight into activity within their S3 buckets.

Imagine your S3 bucket is like a shop in a mall. The beauty of running a shop is that you can see what customers are looking at on your shelves, how long they stay in your shop, and whether they are finding broken items or wanting items that are out of stock. Seeing this enables you to react ensuring you deliver a great customer experience by stocking what your visitors want, when they want it, and helping you to maximize profits.

Log file analysis provides you with this ability for your S3 storage. However, although Amazon Web Services provides comprehensive log files, they are far from simple to interpret. This results in many S3 users not reaping the benefits of obtaining a deep understanding of their customers that is available through this analysis.

The good news is that help is at hand to enable you to obtain this advantage in the shape of S3 log file analysis services. Both open source and commercial solutions are available with the latter being specifically designed for ease of use and to supply the maximum commercial benefits to users.

There is a wealth of data available from log file analysis satisfying those just wanting headline information as well as those looking for deep analysis of their customer's usage.

Here is just a sample of the type of information you can obtain via log file analysis:

Who are your customers and what are they viewing - data available to identify your biggest users (also those costing you the most) as well as what they are viewing. This enables you to make sure you are providing what your visitors want and not what they don't! Can also help you to monitor your S3 costs.

Track a particular customer's visits or the success of a marketing campaign by adding parameters to your communications

Resolve errors occurring within your bucket to maximize your customers experience

The information available from log file analysis is staggering. As more and more people explore, and enjoy, the benefits of Amazon S3, we recommend that users extend the benefits to their business by using log file analysis.

KINDLE FIRE TABLET

Following the success of Kindle e-book reader, Amazon is planned to release its latest electronic device, the Kindle Fire. Quite different from the older versions of Amazon Kindle, this Fire Tablet from Amazon is not only an e-book reader; it is also a tablet computer. The release of this latest tablet computer was announced on September 28, 2011.

The Fire tablet will be the first Amazon Kindle model that does not use Amazon's signature screen display the E Ink Pearl. However, the tablet will use a color 7 inch IPS gorilla glass display. The Fire display resolution is 1,024 x 600 at 169 ppi with 16 million colors. This multi-touch screen also uses the technology of capacitive touch sensitive.

The measurement of this Amazon's Fire tablet will resemble the Kindle Keyboard e-book reader. While Kindle Keyboard measures 7.5 x 4.8 x 0.34 inch, Kindle Fire will measure 7.5 x 4.7 x 0.45 inch. Speaking of weight, the Fire model will be less heavy than the Kindle DX. Fire will only weigh 14.6 ounce.

Using this product, you will acquire a unique browsing experience thanks to the Amazon cloud-accelerated browser. This browser has revolutionary technology which brings you to a faster Internet browsing. Traditionally, to access a page, a website browser will gather 80 files from 13 different domains. This is a heavy work and takes time. Meanwhile, Amazon Silk does not work that way. Amazon Web Services cloud will stack and push the pieces of information gathered to have better, quicker Internet access. This Amazon Silk's latest technology is called the "split browser" architecture.

Upgraded from the old generation of other Kindle models, the Fire model is more improved in terms of internal memory. While other Kindle e-book readers only have 4 GB of memory or holding 3,500 e-books at the most, Kindle Fire will have 8 GB of memory; enough for saving various media contents. 8 GB equals 6,000 e-books, 800 songs, 80 apps, or 10 movies.

The 7 inch color Kindle Fire will be operated by Google's Android 2.3 Gingerbread. It uses the 1 GHz Texas Instruments OMAP 4 dual core processor and 512 MB of RAM. Additionally, it also has type B Micro USB 2.0 port and 3.5 mm stereo jack. To connect to the Internet, the Kindle Fire makes use of the 802.11n Wi-Fi connectivity.

The Amazon Kindle Fire is scheduled to be released on November 15, 2011. To be one of the first people to ever acquire this amazing Amazon product, you can place an early order on Amazon. Kindle Fire will sell US$199 for pre-order.

CHANGES AT AMAZON'S ASTORE

Amazon's aStore is one of the newest affiliates tool provided by Amazon and one of the most successful if we take into consideration profits and the enhancements that are periodically added. Astore is (in their description):

Associates can configure an aStore in Associates Central by navigating through a forms-driven set up process. The store can be built and configured within minutes and Associates only need to copy a line of html code into their web pages. All data will be served from Amazon Web Services and therefore will always be up to date. Once set up, it does not require any maintenance from the Associate.

Recently (and very quietly in fact) they have launched 2 new features:

1. First is a small one, and is a feature that allows you to optionally add to the navigational menu an "About Us" page. Even though is not specified it allows basic HTML formatting to the text (inserting links for example). Basically I see no purpose to that, and perhaps what you could do with that is to provide descriptions to your categories and insert links to some products.

2. The great thing is the addition of "Astore Widgets". Those are JavaScript ads based on your aStore products that can be embedded in other sites. Right now they come in 8 formats and are as customizable as Google's AdSense for example. What do you need to know is the fact that the ads will provide products from your aStore's homepage. If no homepage is set, than the ads will be generic Amazon Ads not related to your store. What is great about the widgets is that on most cases, discounted products are presented and that is made very clear, by that increasing the chance of creating a buy.

Best practice with Astore Widgets:

Even though Astore is great and has a pretty good conversion rate (might depend on your niche though) is not as efficient as Adsense. Because of that, I suggest you not to waste your space with the widgets, but to use it as an alternative to Adsense's Public Ads.

In order to do that, prepare a blank page that:

1. Has the background of your AdSense Ads (as you might know by know, in general try to blend the ads in your page background)

2. Create a centered aligned div where you will place the Astore widget.

3. Upload the created page to a server and provide the link to that page when you generate your AdSense code.

4. Due to the constraint that you can display on the widgets only products from the aStore's Homepage, make sure that you vary its content until you find the most attractive one.

An alternative to this is to use Openads([http://www.openads.org]), and to attach to a zone both AdSense and Astore Widgets.

By doing this you'll have the following benefits:

1. You increase your revenue chances by removing those pesky AdSense public ads.

2. You decrease banner blindness by varying the content.

CLOUD COMPUTING AND SAAS WEB APPS

SaaS (Software as a Service) had almost met its doom in 2001 but it crawled back into contention due to the need of companies to combat with high-cost IT infrastructure. SaaS was revolutionary when it came in, but the expectations were too huge to be fulfilled. SaaS has now managed to smother other new technologies and has several versions in the form of Infrastructure as a service and Platform as a service. SaaS has considerably regained its stature since the dotcom bubble burst and has grown in recent years.

SaaS web apps started out as point solutions and the first players in the market included Up Shot and Sales Net. These solutions provided services related to specific business needs but did not have a huge customer following even though the idea was new and useful. The features were limited and the resources were limited too at their disposal. The competitors who started out offering SaaS solutions offered better features after the dotcom bubble while the originators lost their place of importance and eventually vanished into thin air.

Feasibility of cloud computing and SaaS

The feasibility of cloud computing services has always been undetermined since it is difficult to quantify the benefits as well as its utility in any business context. Business requirements have always mentioned the need for affordable cost but efficient infrastructure but with no solid and structured cloud computing solution in place, it was difficult for businesses to opt for cloud computing. SaaS proved to be an efficient mode of delivery but it is important to know that the IT setup has evolved well over the years and the security measures are better than they were, years before.

Nowadays, there are businesses that are not wary of offshore software testing because of the fantastic setup of offshore service providers. Most are willing to outsource their non-core IT tasks to offshore locations. The cloud has made it possible to save time and money and set up virtual offices to get their tasks done.

Importance of Cloud computing and SaaS web apps

Cloud computing solutions are great for small businesses since they are scalable according to the needs. Additionally, they can even handle the immense workload at cheap monthly prices.

SaaS has grown to several heights and now has become mission-critical too. It has transitioned well from being a unit silo process to a full-fledged enterprise mode of delivery and the SaaS web apps are used for mission-critical purposes related to ERP solutions.

Cloud-computing services consumed from external service providers have taken a huge chunk of the total services offered, according to a Gartner report. The cloud market is preferred today by many with the advent of Amazon Web Services and Microsoft Azure capitalizing on the surge of interest in people for cloud computing. Many organizations have expressed their desired to get into cloud computing by allocating a part of their IT budget for the same. Many of them plan to allocate budget for cloud computing in the near future.

CONCLUSION

An independently managed set of affiliate schemes that allow network members to join any, all, or all of the affiliate schemes is an Affiliate network. It is a club that makes recruiting subsidiaries a straight forward process. This is ideal for portal sites that have a variety of different themes and layouts that can be advertised across a large number of different pages. Merchant is charged by the Affiliate networks to be part of the network and may take a large slice of the affiliate commission. In turn, the affiliate network offers the merchant instant access to hundreds or even thousands of potential affiliates that have already joined the network in the past. In addition, it provides a centralized management console for affiliates to track sales and leads. He is simply an intermediary for a large and complex number of affiliate schemes that all promote themselves alongside their competitors. Commission Junction is a good example of an affiliate network.

o Critical factors for success - To the success of your affiliate marketing strategy, there is always a set of critical factors such as:

Commission that is high: Affiliate marketing efforts are in direct proportion to the commission which they received (relative to competitors' commission levels). An affiliate business model that is successful is based on a reasonable amount of margin available that is shared between the owner of the website and its affiliate at each sale.

o Provision of a unique or distinct product or service - potential affiliates will be attracted to get something slightly different from professional online marketing collateral. If your website is very similar to dozens of other sites, all of which promote its affiliate scheme, why should a potential affiliate sign up for your affiliate scheme instead of your competitors? Therefore, you should really try to sell to a potential affiliate (via your website's affiliate sign-up page), in order to recruit them as an affiliate. It's important to summarize your unique selling points so that they can clearly see an opportunity to make money together.

o Report and quality review - Continuous reassurance through online reports and real-time statistics help encourage affiliates. The more administrative information you are able to provide to an affiliate, the more trust affiliates will have in your ability to strike a deal. As a subsidiary, it's real confidence to see a confirmation email every time a lead or sale is created from the affiliate site. Thus, the more they have more motivation to send more prospective customers in the future.

o Great customer service by the merchant - By providing your professional services to prospects, there is obviously an improvement in your sales conversion ratio. A potential affiliate will look for affiliate schemes that provide good quality conversion ratios with a good reputation in the market. Affiliates should know that each visitor they send to your site has the greatest possibility to make the money you give up effortlessly. There is nothing more incentive for an affiliate than a potential customer or business opportunity that is not followed quickly enough, deleted or mistakenly ignored by the merchant.

o Affiliate recruitment efforts of merchant – Perseverance or time to hire the required number of enthusiastic affiliates is critical. Put these basic questions to yourself... If it takes 6 months to hire 100 affiliates that make 200 sales equivalent to a profit of $100,000. By that time, have you had the chance to make more than 200 sales at that time, also at what profit, if you had only focused on direct selling?

o Affiliate management and software tracking Systems - As a merchant, you must have a profound knowledge of online affiliate tracking programs/software and services to ensure that affiliates are punctually paid, sales allocated fairly, and can start a new affiliate recruitment. If you don't have existing systems, there are many commercial affiliate services available or software packages to provide a comprehensive service to manage and track leads and sales. This is equally crucial for the purpose of accounting. As the greater the size of the affiliate program, the greater the justification for outgoing costs (affiliate commission payments).

Creating an Affiliate Marketing Program - Business Guide

If by now, you're not involved in affiliate marketing, you really are lacking the trick.

Affiliate marketing has evolved from the simple approach that if another website sends traffic/customer to you and that person becomes your client, courtesy demands you say thanks to the other website by giving them a small piece of the cake.

Affiliate marketing is now more complex but the basics are still the same. What you want are many websites to shout about you to their visitors to come and see your merchandise. In return, you pay an appropriate reward for that website based on your business profit and margins.

In this chapter, I will address some of the things a newcomer should consider when setting up an affiliate marketing program:

1. Best commission/reward structure for your business

2. The best network to deal with as regards its affiliate base, for example, the types of affiliates with them, which it tends to attract.

3. Getting visibility on major affiliate sites and their affiliate network.

4. To work on new promotions and incentive programs/schemes to encourage affiliates to promote you instead of your competitors.

In deciding for your business on an affiliate credit structure, the first thing to consider is the cost of hiring your new client, for example, if you spend above $5,000 in a month on marketing, and you hire 100 new clients, then the cost of hiring the new client is $50. You can refer to this with the value of the client's life, that is, if you know it, to see how much commission you can pay to your affiliates.

The primary elucidation for how this is calculated in the following way:

The customer's cost of living will be the average top line profit that each customer brings to you throughout their life.

In order to calculate the value of a customer's lifetime in the best way, perhaps to take a group of customers you have hired within a month's interval and to track their spending in the space of few years, some of these customers will be lost, but will maintain others that need to have a good sample size for the account to be worthy.

Below is a practical example:

Two thousands of clients were hired in the month of February 2016.

Over the next two years, they spent a cumulative $2,000,000, thus you have a customer value of $1000

But

The cost of goods sold was $1,400,000

Fixed business costs were $200,000

Variable business costs were $160,000

So the total profit for these 2000 customers of $240,000 over two years, and profit for each customer of $240/customer.

Obviously, this is an example of a very tough fag package example, but it is worth doing this exercise so that you can then determine the profitability of all your marketing channels by looking at the cost each new business customer pays and comparing it to the value of the customer's life.

However, to stay away from directing the publication model on a very large scale... From this number, you can then decide how much you want to spend for each customer on your marketing (affiliate).

You now know that if you spend $240 per customer acquisition, you get that customer even if you want to make a 50% profit and spend 50% of the customer value, you can spend $120 for each customer acquired.

Now, if you determine the average number of 2,000 customer orders over the two years, you'll know the average order volume by dividing total revenue by total orders.

Assuming that the average number of orders was 4, then you will have an average order size of $500.

Accordingly, if you can spend $60 per new customer order, the commission level for "new" customers can be less than 25%.

However, not all orders are from "new" customers, so you can do one of the following:

1. Take a decision on the average commission in all sales by saying that every customer out of every 4 new customers and therefore you can pay a commission of 6% in general

2. Take a decision to get a higher level of commission on new business orders and a lower level on remaining orders such as 10% and 5% respectively. Although you will need to provide backend site functionality to track different customer segments.

In addition to the cost to the dependent end, you will need to calculate the cost of the network. As a basic guide, this is about 25-35% of the commission paid to affiliates. So if you pay affiliates £1,000 a month, you'll also need to pay your network a fee of around £300 a month, so keep this in mind when setting commission levels.

Always fix your commission levels slightly lower than you can afford so that you have the option of increasing commissions for seasonal promotions, giving high-performance affiliates additional incentives, and so on.

What is my best affiliate network? The amount that affiliate networks want to disclose to you depends on your negotiating skills as well as the potential size of your affiliate networks.

Get close to all the big networks like Buyat, Tradedoubler, Linkshare, Commission Junction, Affiliate Future and lastly, Clickbank has made it clear that you will set up an affiliate marketing program and that you want to get as many information as you can about why you should go with them.

Ask them:

a. What is the number of affiliates they sell for the previous month?

b. In order to compare their size and access them with others

c. What is the number of affiliates that promote merchants in your industry?

d. In order to see how far they reach in your vertical

e. What is the number of revenue they drive into your entire industry for the previous month?

f. So you can judge the level of bottom-line success in your head. Also, you should see (whether it is possible) the percentage detailing revenue through n affiliate, for example, what percentage of revenue is made up of the top 5 affiliates? Is there a substantial amount of long-tail or small affiliate opportunity?

g. The number of new affiliates which they recruited in the previous month?

h. To evaluate the extent of their increased activity and the extent of their participation.

i. In the previous month, what is the number of new merchants they hired?

j. As said before, are they haughty and/or lazy network?

k. Ask them how many traders from your industry are with them? (It's a good idea to deal with the group because there will be a good affiliate base that is prepared to promote you in as much as they are already promoting your competitors.)

l. Which top 5 affiliates are they working with?

m. Which top 5 affiliates are working with them for your industry?

n. What commission will they charge for sales?

o. Can running multiple commission rates be achieved?

p. Can they generate a lead for a fee per lead?

q. What is included in their management fees? How much support and assistance should you expect from them through affiliate employment/reporting/troubleshooting/affiliate updates?

r. What unique technology do they offer?

While you can get a reasonable amount of detail about all of these questions, you should be in a good position to get close to the negotiation stage and play against each other. Obviously, how much leverage you have and how much you can go will depend largely on the size of your business and the type of revenue you will bring to affiliate networks. Make networks excited about marketing and growth plans. Explain your past performance and what your plans are for next year - if you see a growing and growing brand it will stretch further to meet your needs.

On getting to this stage, you will have your preferences, go with the data, the best deal and the intestinal feeling. If you love and connect with people at a real level and trust that they will take your business seriously and will spend time promoting you, then go with them, but only if their commercials are crowded. Get insight with the major affiliates of your market Once you have set up your account and are ready to get started, the first thing you need to do is make a targeted list of affiliates you want to promote. Sort the affiliates on the list as much as possible and then work with the networks to get the best possible real estate on the affiliates' websites.

Induce the affiliate network to give you a list of each affiliate that has sold any competitor to you (in its network) over the past 6 months. Ask your affiliate network to rank affiliates in the order of revenue (without clearly sensitive data) if there is a mess and give you sensitive (unlikely) data and then the best. Make a promotional plan for the first three months and make sure your offers are competitive. Affiliates are companies on their own, so they are only interested in promoting the merchant who can earn them the most money, so if you give them a better% commission and your conversion rate is as good as your competitors or better, you'll quickly win them on. Check out the top EPC affiliates (earnings per click). You'll then need to know how you can give them the opportunity to earn this with you - basically calculating: (site conversion rate x (commission rate per sale X Average order volume).

Make sure that the affiliate network has agreed to give you a unique merchant status for the first month and that it is displayed throughout the website/blog/twitter/facebook and other emails.

Send an email to other affiliates immediately to provide your support at your company, explain your proposal, the terms of the affiliate program (commission rate, etc.) and explain that you have an unbeatable offer for the first month that will have high conversion rates to the sky.

Save some fat in the biggest affiliate promotional spending plan so you can give them something special for a great location on their website.

As soon as you get the top ten onboard and recruit a long tail through email then get on the phone and work down the list to get more and more affiliates on board, there will be many that you can't get and/or who doesn't answer. Do not feel frustrated because this is normal, and affiliates are busy people. Just think about good ways to get their attention and take advantage of all the contacts in your network to help you connect with your affiliates.

Be closely related with the network – acquaint them that you will make them work for their credit/commission. Also, be grateful and appreciate when they're good, but beware of being vaguer after the first wave - you should press at least in the first three months and then, you should start at ease because you have some secure relationships that don't need much maintenance. This applies to both subsidiaries and networks.

Make for a new affiliate promotion for affiliates to promote you instead of your competitors – obviously, this is difficult with no clear correct/false way. There are some rules that I would like to stick to though:

Be fairly straightforward – as has already been mentioned, affiliates are busy, so if you come up with a very complicated though the fun, promotional idea, it may be stopped before you sell it to them.

Keep things new - don't just make the same old offers every month to affiliates, and there won't be any real incentive for them to continue promoting you and try new things for you if they already know how they will work on their site.

If it would be possible, you should focus your promotions on the largest affiliates around their website and what works well for them. For example, if you sell shirts and cushions and one website flies on the cushions, offer them special offers about cushions.

After each promotion, you should use the data you have - find out what works best and try to understand their site usage profile so you can meet their needs.

Make an appearance at affiliate events, make friends in the industry, be generous to people, above all, enjoy yourself so that people see you as socially fun and positive. This will influence your work relationship with them.

Do not go yet; One last thing to do

If you enjoyed this book or found it useful I'd be very grateful if you'd post a short review on it. Your support really does make a difference and I read all the reviews personally so I can get your feedback and make this book even better.

Thanks again for your support!

CPSIA information can be obtained
at www.ICGtesting.com
Printed in the USA
LVHW010750100221
678897LV00004B/819